**New Directions for
Teaching and Learning**

Catherine M. Wehlburg
EDITOR-IN-CHIEF

Interpersonal Boundaries in Teaching and Learning

Harriet L. Schwartz

EDITOR

Number 131 • Fall 2012
Jossey-Bass
San Francisco

INTERPERSONAL BOUNDARIES IN TEACHING AND LEARNING
Harriet L. Schwartz (ed.)
New Directions for Teaching and Learning, no. 131
Catherine M. Wehlburg, Editor-in-Chief

Microfilm copies of issues and articles are available in 16mm and 35mm, as well as microfiche in 105mm, through University Microfilms, Inc., 300 North Zeeb Road, Ann Arbor, MI 48106-1346.

NEW DIRECTIONS FOR TEACHING AND LEARNING (ISSN 0271-0633, electronic ISSN 1536-0768) is part of The Jossey-Bass Higher and Adult Education Series and is published quarterly by Wiley Subscription Services, Inc., A Wiley Company, at Jossey-Bass, One Montgomery Street, Suite 1200, San Francisco, CA 94104-4594. Periodicals postage paid at San Francisco, CA, and at additional mailing offices. POSTMASTER: Send address changes to New Directions for Teaching and Learning, Jossey-Bass, One Montgomery Street, Suite 1200, San Francisco, CA 94104-4594.

New Directions for Teaching and Learning is indexed in CIJE: Current Index to Journals in Education (ERIC), Contents Pages in Education (T&F), Educational Research Abstracts Online (T&F), ERIC Database (Education Resources Information Center), Higher Education Abstracts (Claremont Graduate University), and SCOPUS (Elsevier).

SUBSCRIPTIONS cost $89 for individuals and $275 for institutions, agencies, and libraries in the United States. Prices subject to change.

EDITORIAL CORRESPONDENCE should be sent to the editor-in-chief, Catherine M. Wehlburg, c.wehlburg@tcu.edu.

www.josseybass.com

CONTENTS

FROM THE SERIES EDITOR

About This Publication

Since 1980, *New Directions for Teaching and Learning* (*NDTL*) has brought a unique blend of theory, research, and practice to leaders in postsecondary education. *NDTL* sourcebooks strive not only for solid substance but also for timeliness, compactness, and accessibility.

The series has four goals: to inform readers about current and future directions in teaching and learning in postsecondary education, to illuminate the context that shapes these new directions, to illustrate these new direction through examples from real settings, and to propose ways in which these new directions can be incorporated into still other settings.

This publication reflects the view that teaching deserves respect as a high form of scholarship. We believe that significant scholarship is conducted not only by researchers who report results of empirical investigations but also by practitioners who share disciplinary reflections about teaching. Contributors to *NDTL* approach questions of teaching and learning as seriously as they approach substantive questions in their own disciplines, and they deal not only with pedagogical issues but also with the intellectual and social context in which these issues arise. Authors deal, on one hand, with theory and research and, on the other, with practice, and they translate from research and theory to practice and back again.

About This Volume

This volume focuses on issues of boundaries that are a sometimes-hidden aspect of higher education. Issues of time, space, self-disclosure, and even appropriate relationship boundaries are sometimes so much a part of learning that it is difficult to tell when a boundary has been inappropriately crossed. This volume explores the intricate questions that exist about power, relationships, and privacy.

Catherine M. Wehlburg
Editor-in-Chief

CATHERINE M. WEHLBURG is the assistant provost for Institutional Effectiveness at Texas Christian University.

Editor's Notes

Time, space, availability, self-disclosure, and the nature of relationships—college and university educators frequently face dilemmas and decisions regarding interpersonal boundaries with students. Long-standing questions, such as how much to self-disclose in the classroom and whether to set flexible boundaries with adult students, have been part of the teaching experience for decades. More recent influences such as evolving technology and current generational differences have created a new set of dilemmas. How do we set appropriate expectations regarding e-mail response time in a twenty-four-hour, seven-day-a-week Internet-connected culture? How do we maintain our authority with a generation that views the syllabus as negotiable?

Complex questions about power, positionality, connection, distance, and privacy underlie the aforementioned boundary decision points. This sourcebook provides an in-depth look at interpersonal boundaries between educators and students, giving consideration to the deeper contextual factors and power dynamics that inform how we set, adjust, and maintain boundaries with our students.

"Boundaries are the basic ground rules for the professional relationship. They add structure . . . that provides guidance regarding appropriate actions and interactions. . . . The boundary construct is relevant to all professional relationships that involve a power differential" (Barnett, 2008, p. 5). Seeking to deal with the complexity of interpersonal boundaries, some professors choose to maintain substantial interpersonal distance between themselves and their students while others seek to eliminate the boundary completely (Tom, 1997; Barnett, 2008). Extending the distance between teacher and student can diminish the potential richness of the teacher–student relationship (Tom, 1997; Barnett, 2008). At the same time, failing to acknowledge the power differential or seeking to remove it also reduces teacher effectiveness. In one study, a professor realized that by trying to replace her positional role of professor with that of friend or peer colleague, she was less able to support and guide her graduate students, and her students reported frustration and confusion regarding work expectations (Buck, Mast, Latta, and Kaftan, 2009). In another study (Gardner, Dean, and McKaig, 1989), a professor attempting to eliminate her hierarchical role in a women's studies class realized that when she gave up her position, advanced students assumed power in the room and diminished the participation of other students. Further confirming the need for roles and differentiation, students indicate that boundaries help create a safe space for intellectual risk taking and also maintain the uniqueness of the teacher–student relationship (Schwartz, 2011).

Although boundary decisions are inherent in the lives of educators, the topic is given little attention in the literature. The most commonly discussed boundary situation is that of intimate relationships between teachers and students, a matter sometimes addressed by organizational policy (Tufts University, Office of Equal Opportunity, n.d.; University of Michigan, Office of the Provost, n.d.; University of Queensland, Australia, n.d.). In the scholarly literature, researchers have studied perceptions of boundary violations (Kolbert, Morgan, and Brendel, 2002; Owen and Zwahr-Castro, 2007; Henshaw, 2008) and have provided general frameworks for assessing boundary questions (Tom, 1997; Sumsion, 2000; Barnett, 2008; Johnson, 2008; Buck, Mast, Latta, and Kaftan, 2009). In this sourcebook, we aim to deepen the dialogue regarding interpersonal boundaries between educators and students. Moving beyond the attention-grabbing topic of teachers dating students, we explore the more common boundary questions that faculty confront daily: matters of availability, positionality, shared space, and self-disclosure.

In Chapter One, Booth explores the complexity of student self-disclosure in assignments and classroom activities. She provides strategies for crafting these experiences and responding to students who may self-disclose more than is appropriate. In Chapter Two, McEwan offers a nuanced look at social media and interpersonal boundaries. She helps us think about how to appropriately connect with students in the Web 2.0 context and how to balance student expectations with our own needs in terms of availability and privacy. Next, in Chapter Three, Espinoza describes the concept of generations and shares his research on Millennial values while exploring implications for setting boundaries with this age cohort. In Chapter Four, Booth and I consider the unique boundary questions that emerge when teaching adult learners and use relational practice and deliberate relationship frameworks to process these dynamics and offer strategies. In Chapter Five, Yamashita and I, drawing on Yamashita's research, seek to illuminate boundaries as a cultural construct and to provide strategies for increasing connection and maintaining boundaries with international students. Next, in Chapter Six, Dunn-Haley and Zanzucchi explore boundary challenges in the lives of graduate teaching assistants (GTAs) who are typically beginning their teaching careers and also balancing multiple roles with senior faculty. The authors describe a comprehensive GTA development program that includes significant boundary-related content. In Chapter Seven, Holloway and Alexandre reject conventional ideas about interpersonal boundaries in doctoral education and describe a PhD program that is based on connection and collaboration among students and faculty. In Chapter 8, I provide a synthesis of the volume.

NEW DIRECTIONS FOR TEACHING AND LEARNING • DOI: 10.1002/tl

I would like to thank a number of colleagues who contributed to this sourcebook. I extend my deep appreciation and respect for the chapter authors who have contributed so thoughtfully to this work. In addition, Series Editor Catherine Wehlburg has been a tremendously helpful and enthusiastic guide for this project. Melanie Booth engaged above and beyond her role as a chapter author and helped me consider and reconsider several aspects of this book. And Sandie Turner, Jennifer Snyder-Duch, and Dee Flaherty helped me refine my own writing throughout this project.

Harriet L. Schwartz
Editor

References

Barnett, J. E. "Mentoring, Boundaries, and Multiple Relationships: Opportunities and Challenges." *Mentoring and Tutoring: Partnership in Learning,* 2008, *16*(1), 3–16.

Buck, G. A., Mast, C. M., Latta, M. A. M., and Kaftan, J. M. "Fostering a Theoretical and Practical Understanding of Teaching as a Relational Process: A Feminist Participatory Study of Mentoring a Doctoral Student." *Educational Action Research,* 2009, *17*(4), 505–521.

Gardner, S., Dean, C., and McKaig, D. "Responding to Differences in the Classroom: The Politics of Knowledge, Class, and Sexuality." *Sociology of Education,* 1989, *62*, 64–74.

Henshaw, C. M. "Faculty–Student Boundaries in Associate Degree Nursing Programs." *Journal of Nursing Education,* 2008, *47*(9), 409–416.

Johnson, W. B. "Are Advocacy, Mutuality, and Evaluation Incompatible Mentoring Functions?" *Mentoring and Tutoring: Partnership in Learning,* 2008, *16*(1), 31–44.

Kolbert, J. B., Morgan, B., and Brendel, J. M. "Faculty and Student Perceptions of Dual Relationships Within Counselor Education: A Qualitative Analysis. *Counselor Education and Supervision,* 2002, *41*(3), 193–206.

Owen, P. R., and Zwahr-Castro, J. "Boundary Issues in Academia: Student Perceptions of Faculty–Student Boundary Crossings." *Ethics and Behavior,* 2007, *17*(2), 117–129.

Schwartz, H. L. "From the Classroom to the Coffee Shop: Graduate Students and Professors Effectively Navigate Interpersonal Boundaries. *International Journal of Teaching and Learning in Higher Education,* 2011, *23*(3), 363–372.

Sumsion, J. "Caring and Empowerment: A Teacher Educator's Reflection on an Ethical Dilemma." *Teaching in Higher Education,* 2000, *5*(2), 167–179.

Tom, A. "The Deliberate Relationship: A Frame for Talking About Student–Faculty Relationships." *Alberta Journal of Educational Research,* 1997, *43*(1), 3–21.

Tufts University, Office of Equal Opportunity. "Tufts Policy on Consensual Relationships," n.d. Retrieved from http://oeo.tufts.edu/?pid=18

University of Michigan, Office of the Provost. *University of Michigan Faculty Handbook,* n.d. Retrieved from http://www.provost.umich.edu/faculty/handbook/8/8.D.html

University of Queensland, Australia. *Handbook of Policies and Procedures,* n.d. Retrieved from http://www.uq.edu.au/hupp/index.html?page=24987

HARRIET L. SCHWARTZ, PhD, is an assistant professor in the School of Education at Carlow University in Pittsburgh.

1

How do we navigate the boundary challenges that arise when activities and assignments that are intended to foster and assess authentic and integrated student learning result in students disclosing private information?

Boundaries and Student Self-Disclosure in Authentic, Integrated Learning Activities and Assignments

Melanie Booth

Introduction: When Students Reveal

In one of the first college composition courses I taught, I assigned my students their first essay: "Write an autobiographical essay in which you tell the story of a significant learning experience you had in the last two years. Make sure you also describe how and why it was significant for you." There were, of course, additional requirements, such as the use of relevant rhetorical conventions, formatting, and expected page length. But the gist was this: tell me a story of your life that has significance. I wanted to see if, by writing about themselves, they could authentically engage in the writing process and demonstrate the learning outcomes.

Most of the eighteen- and nineteen-year-old freshmen in the class wrote about relationships that were formed or broken; high school teachers who were particularly influential; courses that shaped their thinking in new ways; travel experiences; or their first cars, lovers, or jobs. But one student (I will call her Julie) turned in an essay that shocked me to my core: she wrote about an accident she caused while driving drunk only nine months earlier that had resulted in the death of her best friend, a passenger in the car. Julie went into great detail (using the appropriate rhetorical conventions) about the accident itself, her grief process, her counseling, her own

New Directions for Teaching and Learning, no. 131, Fall 2012 © Wiley Periodicals, Inc.
Published online in Wiley Online Library (wileyonlinelibrary.com) • DOI: 10.1002/tl.20023

injuries (many of which were visible), and her ongoing angst. She shared with me, in that short essay, a lot about herself, her family situation, and her relationship with her friend and her friend's parents. She *revealed*. How could I assess her writing skills given her story? And how would I give her feedback on her lived experience as written? I did not know what to do.

Several years later, while helping a colleague develop an assignment to assess a particular learning outcome in her sociology of the family course, we devised a final essay prompt that went something like this: "Using the multiple theoretical lenses we have been studying in our course this term, select a family you know well and, in your final essay, apply at least four of the lenses to their familial structure." The professor liked this assignment because it moved away from the lengthy multiple-choice final exam she had been using and allowed her to assess if her students could actually apply and use the theory to analyze a "real" family—a key learning outcome of her course and also of the sociology degree program. Immediately after finals week, the professor called me to let me know something had gone terribly wrong: a couple of her students had written primarily about their own families, had not applied the theoretical lenses at all, and instead had shared many details about their families that were not relevant and, in some cases, were downright disturbing. As she said, "I opened up Pandora's box! I'm going back to my multiple-choice final—this is just too much to deal with!"

As these two examples demonstrate, as faculty in higher education, we may find ourselves reading student work or hearing students' voices in class or in online course discussion boards that reveal a lot of personal information, information that we think might be better kept private, information that may be concerning or even threatening. Furthermore, we might not have intended this to happen. In our attempts to create richer learning activities that are integrated with our students' lived experiences and to assess our students' learning more authentically, we may find that students reveal personal information that raises questions about our boundaries, our roles, and our ethical responsibilities. Many of our students may have certain preconceived notions about what and to whom to self-disclose; for others, these kinds of learning environments may be unknown territory, and thus students navigate them without context or prior experience. Along these lines, one study revealed that students often do not feel certain as to the extent to which they *should* share personal information with their teachers (Keith-Spiegel, Tabachnick, and Allen, 1993). Furthermore, as Lucas (2007) contends, when assignments allow students to choose or customize their own topics, students will, in fact, "disclose their cultures, political leanings, spiritual views, personal biases, habits, hobbies, and social and socioeconomic lives" (p. 368).

Regardless of our intentionality or students' readiness for participating in these kinds of learning activities and assignments, boundary issues may emerge. This chapter reviews the benefits and challenges of fostering authentic, integrated learning; discusses perspectives of privacy, power, and ethics; and identifies approaches for faculty to traverse boundary challenges that may surface in these rich learning environments.

Fostering Authentic, Integrated Learning

The concepts of authentic and integrated learning have been widely applied in higher education over the past several years. Authentic learning is a pedagogical approach for bringing real-world relevance into the classroom with the intent of deepening student engagement, learning, and preparation for life after college. Authentic learning provides students with opportunities to work together to investigate, discuss, and meaningfully understand and apply concepts and relationships with real-world problems and projects that are relevant to the learner (Donovan, Bransford, and Pellegrino, 1999). Likewise, integrated learning is an educational approach that engages students in the "systematic exploration of the relationship between their studies of the 'objective' world and the purpose, meaning, limits, and aspirations of their lives" (Palmer and Zajonc, 2010, p. 10). This pedagogy must take into consideration the need for "carefully crafted relationships of student to teacher, student to student, and teacher to student to subject" (Palmer and Zajonc, 2010, p. 29).

In that authentic and integrated pedagogical approaches connect academic learning to students' lives, several characteristics of these approaches reveal potential challenges with student self-disclosure. Having students apply theory to their own lives and experiences, providing students with opportunities to collaborate with and learn from each other, and asking students to critically reflect on their experiences publicly or privately are but just a few ways in which these kinds of learning approaches can result in students revealing more to us, and potentially to other students, than we anticipated. Indeed, although we may create authentic learning experiences and assignments that *intentionally* request some form of self-disclosure, as I did as a college composition instructor, we also may *unintentionally* design assignments that result in self-disclosure, as did my sociology colleague. Either way, we can quickly find ourselves in uncomfortable positions or significant dilemmas regarding what our students reveal to us and to others in class.

A specific challenge with authentic, integrated learning methods is that they may evoke strong emotions for our students, and many critics of these methods claim that they are problematic because emotions do not belong in the college classroom (Palmer and Zajonc, 2010). These kinds of learning activities can in fact consume the whole person and not just the intellect; they can affect not just the brain but the mind, "which is not an organ but a process" (Palmer and Zajonc, p. 41). But the deep learner engagement that comes from these approaches—engagement that *is* often emotional and that can inspire students to self-disclose—also can

NEW DIRECTIONS FOR TEACHING AND LEARNING • DOI: 10.1002/tl

ultimately result in profound learning outcomes. These approaches thus offer opportunities for transformative learning, when individuals critically reflect on their experiences, beliefs, and assumptions and thus change their frames of reference (Mezirow, 1991, 2000). Bleich (1995), for example, proposes that a full-fledged "pedagogy of disclosure" can be quite significant for learning about power and privilege: "A pedagogy of disclosure needs and asks to know who is in the class with us; it believes that what each person brings to the classroom must become part of the curriculum for that course" (p. 47). This can create what Bleich calls the "contact zone": a point where cultures can meet, clash, converge, and students can ultimately come to understanding.

Regardless of our intention to fully implement a "pedagogy of disclosure" or not, learning activities that we design with authentic and integrated approaches are likely to prompt more self-disclosure than traditional term papers, multiple-choice tests, or factual academic papers (Haney, 2004). Although many of us are committed to authentic and integrated pedagogical approaches because they can, in fact, deepen an individual's or a student group's learning, we also need to be prepared for the reality that some students may have unmet emotional needs; students may need to tell their stories, to share their experiences, to reveal, and to passively or actively seek help. What students reveal may be inextricably linked to their needs to do so (Petronio, 2002). Furthermore, what a student shares or does not share, and which students disclose what kinds of information and how they do so, are aspects of self-disclosure likely influenced by their cultural backgrounds and norms. For example, Delgado Bernal (2002) points out that although "students of color are holders and creators of knowledge, they often feel as if their histories, experiences, cultures, and languages are devalued, misinterpreted, or omitted within formal educational settings" (p. 106).

Students in higher education are also often negotiating three complex tasks simultaneously: learning the academic language and how to participate in the academic conversation, internalizing this language, and then reexternalizing it through writing or other assignments and learning activities (Lucas, 2007). Therefore, even the most careful review of our course assignments and activities may not tell us *why* students disclose what they disclose, but we can predict that somewhere down the line, when we create authentic and integrated learning opportunities, students may self-disclose private information in some form as they are learning their way around our classes and institutions.

Privacy, Power, and the Ethics of Response

When considering the motivations for and effects of students' self-disclosure and resulting interpersonal boundary concerns that may emerge for us, questions about privacy, power, and how we ethically respond come to the surface. First and foremost, as instructors, we operate from our own cultural and social sense of privacy. "Privacy has importance for us because it lets us feel separate from others. It gives us a sense that we are the rightful owners of information about us.... On the other hand, disclosure can give enormous benefits.... The balance of privacy and disclosure has meaning because it is vital to the way we manage our relationships" (Petronio, 2002, p. 2). As indicated earlier, it is important to recognize that students may have different social, generational, cultural, or emotional perspectives that influence how they think about who has access to what information about them and why. We might do well to start by acknowledging that our students' notions of privacy may be quite different from our own. (For further consideration of Millennial students and boundaries, see Chapter Three of this sourcebook.)

Sharing private information most often has negative connotations when it comes to discussion about boundaries between professors and their students, but some students' self-disclosure may be positive in nature and thus support a different purpose. For some students, positive disclosure may help them create closer relationships with people they want to get to know or may promote their own positive affect (Derlega, Anderson, Winstead, and Greene, 2010). When students report their achievements to others, there may be the process of "capitalization" happening whereby the act of sharing a personal positive event provides additional benefit to the person doing the disclosure (Gable, Rice, Impett, and Asher, 2004). The motivational source for sharing private information may be just as complex for positive self-disclosure as it is when students share negative or more complex aspects of their lives, and we therefore are best served when we can be attentive to our own reactions and responses to the information and to the student.

Critics of professors who use learning activities or assignments that call for personal information often cite students' vulnerability as a key argument. Students are vulnerable in one sense because they may be revealing private or sensitive information to other students who may have certain reactions to it; students are vulnerable in another sense in that they may have unmet emotional or mental health needs that are revealed; and students are vulnerable in an entirely different sense in that we instructors are the power holders in the relationship:

> The student-teacher relationship is unique from other work-related relationships. There is an inherent imbalance in the power structure. Students enter this relationship with the understanding that the teacher evaluates student work and provides a grade for class performance. In addition, students enter this relationship likely believing that the teacher possesses a greater understanding of the subject matter... the subtle complexity of the student-teacher relationship necessitates a thoughtful consideration of the teacher's responsibility [Haney, 2004, p. 167].

Particularly when students reveal private information to us, we may feel a need to sustain our position of power to navigate the situation; however, such situations may result in professors misusing the power they have over students whose self-disclosure has made them vulnerable (Ejsing, 2007). Whether students reveal something commendable or something tragic that happened to them, or disclose their political views or religious perspectives that we may either agree or disagree with, the fact that we are in a position of power means we are also in a position of misusing our power. We could assign grades to students unfairly or inequitably, for example, or we could influence our colleagues' treatment of the same students by sharing information the students revealed to us. Ejsing (2007) pointed out the potential challenges of this in her article about teacher self-disclosure, much of which applies to student self-disclosure as well:

> Self-disclosure is to power distribution what a match is to a dry, late-summer forest. It is the seemingly insignificant spark that provokes shifts in power distribution that can generate situations ranging from manageable and harmless to uncontrollable and destructive. In other words, self-disclosure makes class situations unpredictable [p. 241].

The ethics of teaching and response to students is thus another critical consideration to prevent such a self-disclosure spark from becoming an interpersonal or institutional firestorm.

The scholarship of teaching and learning is just beginning to identify the ethical issues related to our rapidly changing teaching and learning cultures, but "the degree of responsibility professors have to their students for addressing these issues is [still] ill-defined territory" (Haney, 2004, p. 167). We make ethical choices in terms of what we want our students to learn as well as how we facilitate their learning. Likewise, we face ethical conundrums when students self-disclose. Do we respond to the content of the self-disclosure or the student who has self-disclosed? Do we refer the student for assistance elsewhere, or might doing so violate confidentiality? How do we grade an assignment that includes self-disclosure, and how do we do so fairly? These kinds of ethical questions come to the surface every time we create and attempt to assess a learning activity that results in a student's self-disclosure.

Haney (2004) suggests that aspects of the ethics code from the American Psychological Association (APA) represent relevant guidance toward considering our ethical responses as instructors and toward managing appropriate interpersonal boundaries with and among our students. Four key principles are particularly relevant:

1. Nonmaleficence, or doing no harm
2. Beneficence, meaning actively promoting the well-being of others

3. Fidelity and Responsibility, encouraging people in positions of power to "manage conflicts that may arise within these relationships to avoid exploitation or harm of others" (Haney, 2004, p. 168)
4. Respect for People's Rights and Dignity, which involves "providing students with sufficient information to make informed choices" (Ibid.)

Haney also points out a fifth principle—the Privacy and Confidentiality standard of the APA—that is quite relevant to instructors as well in that it addresses the need to maintain a balance between protecting confidentiality while also taking into consideration information that could result in individuals harming themselves or others.

Although Haney's suggestions are specific to professors in the fields of psychology, they are generally relevant to all professors in higher education who find themselves struggling with interpersonal boundary questions regarding student self-disclosure. As these guidelines reveal, considering our students' privacy and confidentiality along with the nature of our relationships with them becomes increasingly important as we make our way toward ethical and appropriate responses.

Strategies: Preparing Students and Preparing Ourselves

Although authentic, integrated learning activities and assignments may result in more personal disclosure from our students that challenge boundaries with and among our students, we need not shy away from the deep and significant—often transformative—learning opportunities these pedagogies present. There are several strategies for working from this pedagogical standpoint and being able to work with the student self-disclosure that may result.

Developing Guidelines. If the course includes assignments that explicitly ask for self-disclosure, talking with students at the beginning of the course about self-disclosure and boundaries and the complexity of balancing these when assignments call for self-disclosure can be helpful in preventing challenges. Potentially, students working together with our guidance can create class ground rules or guidelines as well, especially if they are going to be working on the assignments collaboratively. Such an exercise is a good opportunity to:

1. Set the context for the assignment requirements
2. Teach students about our expectations and rationale, the assignment expectations, and expectations of the academic culture in which they are engaged
3. Engage students as a community of participant learners
4. Model transparency

Offering Alternatives. In recognizing that students are learning to navigate our expectations as well as their own sense of what and how much to disclose, we can offer alternative activities or assignments. In my course syllabus, for example, I inform students that because they may be writing about potentially personal and sensitive topics, they have the option of not putting that specific essay through our class peer review process. They will fulfill the course requirements when they participate as an engaged peer reviewer, but they can opt to leave their essay out of the peer review process and get feedback from only me on essays that contain personally sensitive information. In a different course, I remind students to incorporate only personal information that is most relevant to the assigned paper topic, and I let them know that they may propose a different topic as long as the paper will meet the intended learning outcome. Offering such alternatives to students may help them avoid self-disclosing too much or self-disclosing to other students inappropriately.

Ensuring Access to Resources. It might go without saying that we need to ensure that students who do self-disclose personal information that is concerning in nature have access to appropriate resources, such as mental health, legal, or financial counseling. Palmer and Zajonc (2010) remind us of the importance of doing so:

> As a professor, there are places I am not equipped to go with my students, so I must be clear about my limits—clear with myself and with my students. If I invite students to journal about certain topic-related experiences, and I am going to read those journals, I must put boundaries around what they are to submit to me, informing them in advance that I would be guilty of malpractice if I tried to practice therapy. If I get in over my head with a student who does not understand these boundaries, I must partner with people in student affairs who know their way around this territory [p. 41].

Consulting with Others. Haney (2004) suggests that when in doubt about an appropriate response to a concerning self-disclosure, we can consult with trusted colleagues or administrators (and, applying the ethical principles noted earlier, maintain the confidentiality of the student when doing so). What happens in our classrooms and with our students may not be areas that we are comfortable talking about with other faculty or administrators. However, especially when what a student reveals is particularly concerning, we may very well need to talk with other people to check our thinking about the best course of action given institutional policies, the Family Educational Rights and Privacy Act, and cases of precedence.

Assessing Learning. Focusing our assessment methods on whether students are actually demonstrating the intended learning outcomes of an assignment or the course can help us avoid the conundrum of being positively or negatively influenced by information students might self-disclose within the assignment. Developing a rubric that communicates our criteria and expectations, and sharing that rubric with students before they prepare their assignments, can help everyone stay focused on what students need to demonstrate related to the specific learning outcomes.

Practicing Empathy and Respect. When designing learning activities and assignments that will engage the whole student, we should be prepared to practice empathy and respect when self-disclosure that challenges our comfort with boundaries does occur. "With empathy and respect, we create contact rather than distance, enabling both ourselves and our students to see each other as 'us' rather than 'them'" (Lucas and DeGenaro, 2007, p. 395). This is particularly important in authentic and integrated learning situations where relationships are critical to the learning process. It is also crucial when the student is in crisis. As Haney (2004) reminds us, there are times when it may be necessary to temporarily step outside one's boundaries of competence and comfort until a student in crisis is connected with appropriate resources. An empathic and respectful response to students can lend great support during these times, opening up the way for resolution.

Furthermore, we must be able and willing to genuinely acknowledge and value the histories and stories *all* of our students bring to our classes (Delgado Bernal, 2002, p. 121). If we believe that our students' learning is enhanced by having them reflect on lived experience or connect theory to "real-life" situations and share these ideas with others, then we also must value their contributions. Although students' diverse backgrounds, perspectives, and experiences may be challenging for us to incorporate or to navigate during course discussions or collaborative learning activities, ensuring that all voices are heard and respecting *that* our students contribute their perspectives (even if we do not agree with *what* they contribute) is all part of creating a rich learning atmosphere—for our students and ourselves.

Conclusion

Authentic and integrated learning pedagogies show great promise in supporting deep and potentially transformative learning opportunities for our students, in assessing student learning more meaningfully, and in engaging our students in their learning and the learning of others, including ourselves, in new ways. The potential boundary challenges associated with student self-disclosure can be proactively managed and retroactively addressed with careful thought and action and with empathy, respect, and ethical responses toward our students. Shying away from authentic, integrated assignments that may result in self-disclosure and moving to "safer" assignments that may not invoke self-disclosure of any kind need not be the solution to our own discomfort. According to Palmer and Zajonc (2010), the question we professors and our institutions need to reflect on accordingly is this: "whether we want higher education to be about life" (p. 36).

References

Bleich, D. "Collaboration and the Pedagogy of Disclosure." *College English*, 1995, *57*(1), 43–61.

Delgado Bernal, D. "Critical Race Theory, Latino Critical Theory, and Critical Race-Gendered Epistemologies: Recognizing Students of Color and Holders and Creators of Knowledge. *Qualitative Inquiry*, 2002, *8*, 105–126. Retrieved from http://qix.sage-pub.com/content/8/1/105

Derlega, V. J., Anderson, S., Winstead, B. A., and Greene, K. "Positive Disclosure Among College Students: What Do They Talk About, to Whom, and Why? *Journal of Positive Psychology*, 2010, *6*(2), 119–130.

Donovan, M. S., Bransford, J. D., and Pellegrino, J. W. (eds.). *How People Learn: Bridging Research and Practice*. Washington, D.C.: National Academy Press, 1999.

Ejsing, A. "Power and Caution: The Ethics of Self-Disclosure. *Teaching Theology and Religion*, 2007, *10*(4), 235–243.

Gable, S. L., Rice, H. T., Impett, E. A., and Asher, E. R. "What Do You Do When Things Go Right? The Intrapersonal and Interpersonal Benefits of Sharing Positive Events." *Journal of Personality and Social Psychology*, 2004, *87*, 228–245.

Haney, M .R. "Ethical Dilemmas Associated with Self-Disclosure in Student Writing." *Teaching of Psychology*, 2004, *31*(4), 167–171.

Keith-Spiegel, P. C., Tabachnick, B. G., and Allen, M. "Ethics in Academia, Students' Views of Professors' Actions." *Ethics and Behavior*, 1993, *3*, 149–162.

Lucas, J. "Getting Personal: Responding to Student Self-Disclosure." *Teaching English in the Two Year College*, 2007, *34*(4), 367–379.

Lucas, J., and DeGenaro, W. "Student Self Disclosure." *Teaching English in the Two Year College*, 2007, *34*(4), 394–395.

Mezirow, J. *Transformative Dimensions of Adult Learning*. San Francisco: Jossey-Bass, 1991.

Mezirow, J. *Learning as Transformation: Critical Perspectives on a Theory in Progress*. San Francisco: Jossey-Bass, 2000.

Palmer, P., and Zajonc, A. *The Heart of Higher Education: A Call to Renewal*. San Francisco: Jossey-Bass, 2010.

Petronio, S. *Boundaries of Privacy: Dialectics of Disclosure*. Albany: State University of New York Press, 2002.

MELANIE BOOTH, EdD, is the dean of learning and assessment and director of the Center for Experiential Learning and Assessment at Marylhurst University in Oregon.

2

This chapter explores the use of social media in the higher education classroom highlighting potential issues for student–faculty boundary management and providing suggestions for praxis.

Managing Boundaries in the Web 2.0 Classroom

Bree McEwan

In recent years, many faculty members have been intrigued by potential academic applications of social media to higher education (McLoughlin and Lee, 2007; Heiberger and Harper, 2008; Ajjan and Hartshorn, 2008; Grosseck, 2009; Schwartz, 2009; Croxall, 2010; Karl and Peluchette, 2011). Social media has the potential to enhance communication with students (Hewitt and Forte, 2006; Thompson, 2008; Hughes, 2009) and increase engagement with course material (Junco, 2011). However, because most social media platforms are not specifically designed for classroom use, the use of these technologies introduces communication challenges that may not be present with other types of education technology.

Teaching with Social Media

Social media refers to Web-based communication technologies such as social networking sites (SNSs), wikis, blogging, microblogging, and multimedia sharing sites that allow users to connect, create, and share content with other users. SNSs allow individuals to build a profile and share messages and information with others whom they connect with within the system (boyd and Ellison, 2007). Popular SNSs, such as Facebook, LinkedIn, Academia.edu, and Google+, are open to the public. However, some SNSs, such as Ning.com, are closed systems specifically intended for academic use. Wikis are Web sites that allow multiple users to edit Web pages and documents (Anderson, 2007). Instructors can use wikis to maintain course

New Directions for Teaching and Learning, no. 131, Fall 2012 © Wiley Periodicals, Inc.
Published online in Wiley Online Library (wileyonlinelibrary.com) • DOI: 10.1002/tl.20024

frequently asked questions (FAQs), encourage discussion, and post resources (Grosseck, 2009). Blogs are online journals that individuals or groups can keep on any topic (Anderson, 2007). Course blog postings often consist of longer posts by one or more students. Other students are then invited to comment, creating a conversation between the original author(s) and the audience (Anderson, 2007). Blogs can be used to help students garner real-world writing experience and facilitate peer and faculty feedback (Grosseck, 2009). A form of blogging called microblogging consists of publishing very brief messages (Grosseck and Holotescu, 2008). Currently, one of the most popular microblogging sites is Twitter (www .twitter.com). Hashtags, retweets, and use of the @ symbol, which directs messages to specific receivers, help users contextualize and make meaning from the stream of information. Students can follow the instructor and experts, share resources, post related links, and ask questions about the course materials (Dunlap and Lowenthal, 2009; Grosseck, 2009). Finally, multimedia sharing of online videos, photographs, and podcasts on sites such as YouTube.com or Flickr.com are also considered social media (Anderson, 2007). Multimedia sharing is the most common course-related use of social media; Moran, Seaman, and Tinti-Kane (2011) found that 80 percent of faculty members reported using some type of online video. Assigning students to view digital images, listen to podcasts, or post their own multimedia projects are also common pedagogical uses of social media (Grosseck, 2009; Moran, Seaman, and Tinti-Kane, 2011).

College students and faculty are familiar with social media (Lampe, Ellison, and Steinfield, 2008; Subrahmanyam, Reich, Waechter, and Espinoza, 2008). The Pew Center for Internet Research reported that 86 percent of undergraduates age 18 to 29 use an SNS (Smith, Rainie, and Zickuhr, 2011) with 45 percent visiting an SNS every day (Lenhart, Purcell, Smith, and Zickuhr, 2010). Similarly, the Babson Survey Research Group in conjunction with Pearson found that 75 percent of faculty members used a social media site in the past month (Moran, Seaman, and Tinti-Kane, 2011).

Given the saturation of social media in university communities and the ability of social media to facilitate knowledge sharing to a user-defined mass audience (O'Sullivan, 2005), some faculty members are turning toward social media to disseminate information, connect with students, create learning opportunities, and encourage deeper student engagement with course material (Thompson, 2008; Hughes, 2009; Grosseck, 2009; Ophus and Abbitt, 2009; Ossiansson, 2010; Espuny, Gonzalez, Fleixa, and Gibbert, 2011; Junco, 2011; Moran, Seaman, and Tinti-Kane, 2011).

Students and faculty alike have reported they would enjoy the ease and convenience of communicating with each other via Facebook (Ophus and Abbitt, 2009). Students can use social media to reach out for mentoring, for extra help on assignments, or to stay in touch with professors once the course has ended (Bosch, 2009; Woodward, Jones, and Blackey, 2010; Helvie-Mason, 2011). Increased communication via social media may also improve instructor–student relationships (Schroeder, Minocha, and Schneider, 2010). In-class interaction may be improved by social media use as students may find it easier to engage and interact with lecturers in person after interacting with them online (Bosch, 2009; Sturgeon and Walker, 2009; Helvie-Mason, 2011). Students who have access to a professor's SNS profile may view him or her more favorably in terms of trustworthiness and perceived caring (Mazer, Murphy, and Simonds, 2009). Classroom performance for these students may also be improved; those who had viewed an instructor's Facebook page with a high amount of disclosure report higher levels of motivation, affective learning, and positive evaluations of classroom climate (Mazer, Murphy, and Simonds, 2007). Mazer, Murphy, and Simonds (2009) argue that Facebook allows teachers to "present themselves ... as individuals who function outside of the classroom in social situations unlike the traditional face-to-face classroom environments" (p. 180). Increased communication via social media may cause students to enjoy those instructors' classes more as increased self-disclosure typically leads to reduced uncertainty and higher degrees of liking (Berger and Calabrese, 1975).

Social media can help increase student engagement with course material by facilitating interesting assignments, collaborative learning, and additional channels to disseminate information (Roblyer and others, 2010; Schroeder, Minocha, and Schneider, 2010; Moran, Seaman, and Tinti-Kane, 2011). For example, microblogging has been associated with increased student engagement and improved academic outcomes (Junco, Heiberger, and Loken, 2010; Junco, 2011; Schirmer, 2011). A. Jones (2011) found that when Twitter was used in a social manner for course discussion, student engagement, attendance, and in-class contribution increased. Blogs can be used for unique writing assignments and course discussion (Kupetz, 2010). Multimedia sites allow students to share visual course projects with both the class and a wider public audience (see Wesch, n.d., for exemplars).

Social media use may positively affect peer relationships within a particular course. Students can use social media to share course projects, organize group work, and provide peer feedback (Dunlap and Lowenthal, 2009; Madge, Meek, Wellens, and Hooley, 2009). Schroeder, Minocha, and Schneider (2010) found that academic social media use increased community spirit among students. However, instructors may want to moderate this type of usage, as Selwyn (2007) has warned that student-to-student social media communication may devolve to kvetching about assignments and instructors.

Student–Faculty Boundaries

As demonstrated, social media may provide a potentially useful pedagogical tool. However, concerns exist that interaction on social media platforms may blur the traditional boundaries of the student–teacher relationship

(Bosch, 2009; Madge, Meek, Wellens, and Hooley, 2009; Sturgeon and Walker, 2009). Petronio (2002) argues that boundaries vary based on the relationship of the communicator and the information being exchanged or withheld. Boundaries are not static structures to be crossed or violated but rather negotiated discursive membranes of varying degrees of permeability protecting or revealing information (Petronio, 2002). Boundaries and boundary negotiations are based in part around social norms regarding appropriateness of the amount and type of disclosure in student–faculty relationships (Barnett, 2008; Petronio, 2002). In the case of the student–faculty relationship, there is some expectation that while faculty and students will share in depth in relation to course material, personal information will be more restricted. There is evidence that students expect a thickening of information boundaries in regard to personal information in student–faculty relationships (Holmes, Rupert, Ross, and Shapera, 1999; Owen and Zwahr-Castro, 2007).

Because of the social intention and because information can easily traverse between contexts and various audiences (boyd, 2011; McEwan, 2011), social media may make it difficult for both faculty and students to maintain rigid and thick boundary structures around personal information. Shifting the site of boundary negotiation from the classroom to the Internet creates new challenges. Both faculty and students may disclose information via social media that they intend for audiences other than students or teachers. Disclosures posted to the Internet are often received by unintended audiences (boyd, 2011). Student pictures of last night's wild party might be viewed by faculty; a faculty member's political activity could end up in front of student eyes. When student–faculty boundaries become more porous due to the use of social media, both faculty and students can become confused about appropriate roles and feel uncomfortable with disclosure levels. In addition, professional objectivity can be affected (Owen and Zwahr-Castro, 2007).

One step that educators have considered in developing social media applications for the classroom is to make the use of these new technologies optional for students (Helvie-Mason, 2011). The hope is to avoid forcing students into uncomfortable situations. However, this may not be the best course of action. Junco (2011) found improvements in student engagement only for classes where Twitter usage was made mandatory; no improvement was found in classes where Twitter was optional. If an instructor intends to make social media an assignment, it seems unlikely that such an assignment can be optional. Also, if instructors want to use social media to convey instructions and announcements, they must consider how students who do not use the social media platform will receive that information. Finally, simply placing the onus of the decision whether to use social media on students does not free instructors of their responsibility to provide safe and ethical spaces for students both on- and offline. Instructors who choose to use social media for academic purposes should take steps to educate themselves about boundary challenges and provide a learning environment that is accessible to all of their students.

Boundary Regulation Challenges

The following strategies will help faculty consider and maintain interpersonal boundaries with students in social media spaces.

Avoiding Space Invasion. The initial challenge of using social media for pedagogical purposes is determining what type of space will be used and how students will be invited into that space. Instructors should avoid creating creepy treehouses, or situations "in which an authority figure or an institutional power forces those below him/her into social or quasi-social situations" (Stein, 2008, para. 2). Faculty use of social media may create such situations if students feel forced to engage socially with faculty. This effect can be magnified if students dislike the faculty member requesting to interact via social media; students report being irritated and suspicious if a disliked faculty member tries to connect with them via social media (Karl and Peluchette, 2011).

However, I. B. Jones (2010) argues: "The creepy treehouse problem is largely one of bad pedagogy. There's a problem when faculty assume that the contribution of social media to student engagement is produced through hanging out with students online, rather than in using those media to make possible new kinds of learning" (para. 6).

Rather than trying to force a potentially unwanted social relationship with students in the name of pedagogy, professors should choose the right platform with which to engage in professional communication via social media. Locke's (2007) typology of social media may help instructors make appropriate choices. According to Locke, individuals consider mediums such as instant messages (IM) or texting to be *secret* spaces. Although the communication here is written and semipermanent, generally individuals perceive that only the sender and the intended receiver of these communications will be privy to the messages. The next category is *group* spaces. Group spaces include SNSs. Again, although the communications could be public, students generally expect that the communication will be limited to members of a group whom they have selected to be receivers. The third category is *publishing* spaces: blogs, microblogging, wikis, and online video. Although audiences in these spaces can be restricted, individuals generally intend their messages for a wider audience. The fourth category is *performance* spaces, where individuals can experiment with various identities. These spaces include Web sites such as Second Life or online role playing games. The fifth category, *participation* spaces, includes online meetings, marketplaces, and events. Locke's final category is *watching spaces*, which includes lectures where students anticipate passive message reception.

Faculty intrusion into secret and group spaces, as defined by Locke (2007), may be perceived as entering creepy treehouse territory and violating norms of the faculty–student relationship because students expect to be able to restrict group membership. Indeed, Hewitt and Forte's participants (2006) indicated that they perceived Facebook as a "student environment." However, using an SNS where the group is specifically designed to be the classroom group may allow some of the benefits of using SNSs in the classroom while avoiding intruding on students' virtual social space (and vice versa, by keeping students out of instructors' personal virtual space). Faculty members who simply want to establish online connections with students might consider using a network such as LinkedIn, which is designed for professional connections. SNSs such as Ning.com may work better for instructional purposes. However, students may be less likely to use a university- or course-only SNS than an established, general SNS (Oradini and Saunders, 2008; Espuny, Gonzalez, Lleixa, and Gisbert, 2011; Junco, 2011). To use platforms such as Facebook while avoiding creepy treehouses, instructors might set up group pages that students can choose to join (Helvie-Mason, 2011). This method allows students and faculty to communicate via the SNS but does not allow access to each others' profile information.

Instructors should also think beyond SNSs for pedagogy facilitated by social media. Publishing and performance spaces may be better suited for coursework. Blogging, microblogging, wikis, and multimedia sharing allow instructors to tap into benefits of social media, including creating unique assignments, peer review, public presentation, and instructor feedback. At the same time, instructors avoid creepy treehouse creation because students do not expect these spaces to be private. Thus, students are unlikely to feel that they are being forced to socialize with faculty. For this reason, publishing and performance spaces may be more academically appropriate than spaces that are understood to be primarily social. Indeed, Moran, Seaman, and Tinti-Kane (2011) found that when faculty use social media for academic purposes, they are likely to choose publishing spaces; most common choices are online video followed by podcasts, blogs, and wikis. Microblogging may prove to be a fertile platform for classroom purposes (Grosseck and Holotescu, 2008; Junco, Heilberger, and Loken, 2010; Junco, 2011; Schirmer, 2011). Microblogging is viewed as a publishing space but, like SNSs, allows for continuous communication between students and faculty (Ebner, Lienhardt, Rohs, and Meyer, 2010).

Managing Disclosure. Instructors and students may find it challenging to manage self-disclosure competently via social media. Although the faculty–student relationship is primarily a professional relationship, it is one that benefits from some personal disclosure. Self-disclosure on the part of instructors has been shown to create an immediate classroom environment (McBride and Wahl, 2005). Immediacy behaviors in the classroom—those that communicate closeness and warmth (Mehrabian, 1969)—are associated with positive student outcomes, including increased motivation, engagement, and learning (Plax, Kearney, McCroskey, and Richmond,

1986; Christophel, 1990; Christensen and Menzel, 1998; Cayanus, Martin, and Goodboy, 2009). Self-disclosures that improve student outcomes could easily take place via social media. In this way instructors could utilize social media to create an immediate relationship with their students. As noted, Mazer, Murphy, and Simonds (2007, 2009) found that disclosure of personal information on Facebook is related to increases in affective learning, student motivation, and students' rating of instructor trustworthiness.

However, the link between instructor disclosure and positive student outcomes is not a direct linear relationship. Studies have found that overly personal or negative disclosures may lead to negative student perceptions of the faculty member (Cayanus, Martin, and Goodboy, 2009). Students may view faculty discussing personal problems and information as inappropriate for the student–faculty relationship (Holmes, Rupert, Ross, and Shapera, 1999; Owen and Zwahr-Castro, 2007).

Instructors should understand that positive student outcomes related to disclosure are based on appropriately managing boundary tensions regarding disclosure (Baxter and Sahlstein, 2000; Petronio, 2002). Instructors should be careful about disclosing very personal or negative information to students as this information may be inappropriate for such an audience. However, as noted previously, disclosure of some information on social media can lead to students viewing a professor as friendly, approachable, and trustworthy. Instructors who choose to self-disclose to students through SNSs, blogging, or microblogging should recognize this dialectical tension and attempt to manage accordingly. Disclosures probably should be kept at the orientation level, which includes small talk, disclosure of likes and dislikes, hobbies, and so on (Altman and Taylor, 1973). Disclosures that are relevant to the course material are also more likely to be received positively by students (Cayanus, Martin, and Goodboy, 2009).

Individual instructors will have to determine the amount of personal disclosure they are comfortable with and feel will be appropriate for their students. In this sense, social media can be a useful tool for disclosure because messages can be carefully considered and crafted before being posted, if one resists the typical quick pace of tools such as Twitter. It is important to recognize that inappropriate posted disclosures are likely permanent and can be transmitted to unintended audiences.

Friending Fairly. Another issue faculty members may have when using social media to communicate with students is setting guidelines on how they choose to connect with students. Some faculty members have an open door policy on their social media accounts and friend all comers. Others choose to keep their profiles private from all students. Others create policies (informally or formally) that find some middle ground between these options. The choice that works for a particular faculty member will depend on her or his comfort level and the type of information she or he is communicating online. Although some (Maranto and Barto, 2009; De Luca,

2010) have discouraged faculty members from connecting with students in any way on social media, there is nothing inherent about the medium that makes such connections problematic. Rather, it is the communication choices one makes on a medium that can create blurred boundary lines and potentially uncomfortable situations. Research suggests that faculty–student interaction outside the classroom has a generally positive impact on students in terms of student engagement with the university community and increased academic achievement (Pascarella and Terenzini, 1991; Astin, 1993). Social media provides an additional channel where faculty and students can communicate. In some cases, students may be more willing to reach out to faculty online as the medium may feel less immediate and threatening. The research of Mazer, Murphy, and Simonds (2007, 2009) suggests that faculty–student online interaction may produce favorable results for students.

However, there are issues that faculty members should carefully consider when choosing to connect with individual students via social media. Combining professional and personal information can affect professional objectivity (Owen and Zwahr-Castro, 2007) and raise ethical concerns when connections are made with some students but not others (Bryer and Chen, 2010). On one hand, professors may be more likely to connect via social media and provide preferential treatment and extra communication to students they find likable (Mendez and others, 2009). However, engaging with only some students through social media may lead to favoritism and extra opportunities for those students at the expense of others. On the other hand, instructors may engage in harsher penalties for students whose personal information they find less appealing or even problematic. Woodward, Jones, and Blackey (2010) noted that "students invariably do not give any consideration to being a *Friend* when using Facebook, and publishing their status updates and comments" (p. 76). Students may also neglect to consider the timing of their postings (Woodward, Jones, and Blackey, 2010). Postings that appear during class time or late at night prior to a morning class may give instructors pause.

Faculty members should set guidelines for themselves regarding how they will connect with students *prior* to making such connections (Schwartz, 2009). These guidelines should reflect the faculty members' own comfort level as well as the content of the medium in question. Directing students to a blog or microblog account where faculty members present information and articles in their field may be an excellent way for interested students to develop a deeper connection to their coursework. Directing students to a blog that primarily focuses on a faculty member's personal life or complaints will likely be viewed as inappropriate.

Faculty members should be particularly careful about their connections on SNS with students. Given the social nature of these sites, it can be tricky to combine personal and professional connections. The personal messages prevalent on SNSs, referencing, celebrating, or complaining about ones' family or social life, are the very messages that students find inappropriate coming from faculty members. Owen and Zwahr-Castro (2007; see also Holmes, Rupert, Ross, and Shapera, 1999) found that students were concerned about faculty members attempting to form personal relationships with students as well as receiving or being asked to disclose personal information. As noted previously, considerations of the platform are important. A faculty member might be willing to connect to students on a site such as LinkedIn, which is designed for professional connections, but bar students from a Facebook account to restrict access to more personal information. Some faculty members may be willing to friend graduate students but not undergraduates due to the closer relational expectations of graduate students. Other faculty members will friend students only once they are no longer in a position to evaluate them, either when the course has ended or the students have graduated from the institution. The norms of one's department and institution are important to consider as well. Woodward, Jones, and Blackey (2010) noted that in their discipline (geography), it seemed more natural to friend students who had already been in the field as faculty, and students tended to develop close relationships after working together abroad.

In making their decisions regarding connecting to students via social media, faculty members should be aware of the power differential that exists between themselves and their students and make choices accordingly. In cases where the medium is not purely course related, faculty members should wait for students to reach out and friend or follow them rather than attempting to create the connection. Students may feel as if they must accept a faculty member's request as it is difficult to refuse requests from higher-status individuals (Brown and Levinson, 1987). Reaching out to students in this way may create a creepy treehouse situation where students feel forced to engage with the faculty member in a social situation. Students may feel that such requests are tantamount to spying and a violation of their privacy (Connell, 2009; Malesky and Peters, 2011).

Set Availability Expectations. Faculty members may be concerned about the time required to engage with students via social media (Schroeder, Minocha, and Schneider, 2010; Moran, Seaman, and Tinti-Kane, 2011). Although the continuous communication provided by social media may be pedagogically useful, faculty members are concerned at having to be on-call via Facebook or Twitter to students at all times (Grosseck and Holotescu, 2008; Sturgeon and Walker, 2009). Those who choose to require students to use social media for assignments or even just casually connect with students through social media should set clear expectations regarding how often and when they will respond to student messages. Faculty members may consider letting students know approximately how often they check particular accounts or request that students indicate how quickly they require a response. For example, a faculty member might allow contact via SNS messaging but request that students allow at least twenty-four hours before they expect a return message. Ground rules regarding social media contact should be established early on in a faculty–student relationship (and placed in the course syllabus, where appropriate). Otherwise, Millennial students have a tendency to expect immediate return responses (Lenhart, Ling, Campbell, and Purcell, 2010). (For further exploration of boundaries and Millennial students, see Chapter Three of this sourcebook.)

Conclusion

Social media has captured the attention of educators and provides exciting new ways to engage students in course material. However, instructors and students alike must exercise caution in renegotiating the boundaries of the professional faculty–student relationship or risk creating uncomfortable situations that are not conducive to learning. By taking care to understand the goals of different types of social media and utilizing spaces that allow students and instructors to achieve learning objectives while maintaining appropriate boundaries, faculty members may be able to open up new lines of communication and engage in innovative pedagogy.

References

Ajjan, H., and Hartshorne, R. "Investigating Faculty Decisions to Adopt Web 2.0 Technologies: Theory and Empirical Tests." *Internet and Higher Education*, 2008, *11*(2), 71–80.

Altman, I., and Taylor, D. *Social Penetration: The Development of Interpersonal Relationships.* New York: Holt, Rinehart, and Winston, 1973.

Anderson, P. "What is Web 2.0? Ideas, Technologies, and Implications for Education." *JISC Report*, 2007. Retrieved from www.jisc.ac.uk./media/documents/techwatch/tsw0701b.pdf

Astin, A. W. *What Matters in College?* San Francisco: Jossey-Bass, 1993.

Barnett, J. E. "Mentoring, Boundaries, and Multiple Relationships: Opportunities and Challenges." *Mentoring and Tutoring: Partnership in Learning*, 2008, *16*(2), 3–16.

Baxter, L. A., and Sahlstein, E. M. "Some Possible Directions for Future Research." In S. Petronio (ed.), *Balancing the Secrets of Private Disclosures*. Mahwah, NJ: Lawrence Erlbaum, 2000.

Berger, C., and Calabrese, R. "Some Explorations in Initial Interaction and Beyond: Toward a Developmental Theory of Interpersonal Communication. *Human Communication Research*, 1975, *1*(1), 99–112.

Bosch, T. E. "Using Online Social Networking for Teaching and Learning: Facebook Use at the University of Cape Town." *Communicatio: South African Journal of Communication Theory and Research*, 2009, *35*(2), 185–200.

boyd, d. m. "Social Network Sites as Networked Publics." In Z. Papachrissi (ed.), *A Networked Self: Identity, Community, and Culture on Social Network Sites.* New York: Routledge, 2011.

boyd, d. m., and Ellison, N. B. "Social Network Sites: Definition, History, and Scholarship." *Journal of Computer-Mediated Communication*, 2007, *13*(1), 210–230.

Brown, P., and Levinson, S. *Politeness: Some Universals in Language Use.* Cambridge, U.K.: Cambridge University Press, 1987.

Bryer, T. A., and Chen, B. "The Use of Social Media and Networks in Teaching Public Administration." In C. Wankel (ed.), *Cutting-Edge Social Media Approaches to Business Education: Teaching with LinkedIn, Facebook, Twitter, Second Life, and Blogs.* Bingley, U.K.: Emerald Group, 2010.

Cayanus, J. L., Martin, M., and Goodboy, A. K. "The Relation Between Teacher Self-Disclosure and Student Motives to Communicate." *Communication Research Reports,* 2009, *26*(2), 105–133.

Christensen, L. J., and Menzel, K. E. "The Linear Relationship Between Student Reports of Teacher Immediacy Behaviors and Perceptions of State Motivation, and of Cognitive, Affective, and Behavioral Learning." *Communication Education,* 1998, *47*(1), 82–90.

Christophel, D. M. "The Relationships Among Teacher Immediacy Behaviors, Student Motivation, and Learning." *Communication Education,* 1990, *39*(4), 323–340.

Connell, R. S. "Academic Libraries, Facebook, and MySpace, and Student Outreach: A Survey of Student Opinion." *Libraries and the Academy,* 2009, *9*(1), 25–36.

Croxall, B. "Reflection on Teaching with Social Media." *Chronicle of Higher Education,* June 7, 2010. Retrieved from http://chronicle.com/blogs/profhacker/reflections -on-teaching-with-social-media/24556

DeLuca, J. "One New Friend Request … from My Professor?" *USA Today,* August 13, 2010. Retrieved from www.usatodayeducate.com/staging/index.php/blog/one -new-friend-request-from-my-professor

Dunlap, J. C., and Lowenthal, P. R. "Tweeting the Night Away: Using Twitter to Enhance Social Presence." *Journal of Information Systems Education,* 2009, *20*(2), 129–137.

Ebner M., Lienhardt C., Rohs, M., and Meyer, I. "Microblogs in Higher Education—A Chance to Facilitate Informal and Process-Oriented Learning." *Computers and Education,* 2010, *55*(1), 92–100.

Espuny, C., Gonzalez, J., Lleixa, M., and Gisbert, M. "University Students' Attitudes Towards and Expectations of the Educational Use of Social Networks." *Revista de Universidad y Sociodad del Conocimiento (RUSC),* 2011, *8*(1), 186–199.

Grosseck, G. "To Use or Not Use Web 2.0 in Higher Education?" *Procedia: Social and Behavioral Sciences,* 2009, *1*(1), 478–482.

Grosseck, G., and Holotescu, C. "Can We Use Twitter for Educational Activities?" Paper presented at the fourth International Scientific Conference, eLearning and Software for Education, Bucharest, 2008. Retrieved from http://adl.unap.ro/else/

Heiberger, G., and Harper, R. *Have You Facebooked Astin Lately? Using Technology to Increase Student Involvement.* New Directions for Student Services, no. 124. San Francisco: Jossey-Bass, 2008. doi:10.1002/ss293

Helvie-Mason, L. "Facebook, 'Friending,' and Faculty–Student Communication." In C. Wankel (ed.), *Teaching Arts and Sciences with the New Social Media: Cutting-Edge Technologies in Higher Education* (vol. 3). Bingley, U.K.: Emerald Group, 2011.

Hewitt, A., and Forte, A. "Crossing Boundaries: Identity Management and Student/ Faculty Relationships on the Facebook." Paper presented at the annual meeting of the CSCW, Banff, Alberta, Canada, November 4–8, 2006.

Holmes, D. L., Rupert, P. A., Ross, S. A., and Shapera, W. E. "Student Perceptions of Dual Relationships Between Faculty and Students." *Ethics and Behavior,* 1999, *9*(2), 79–107.

Hughes, A. "Higher Education in a Web 2.0 World." *JISC Report,* March 2009. Retrieved from www.jisc.ac.uk/media/documents/publication/heweb20rptv1.pdf

Jones, A. (2011). "How Twitter Saved My Literature Class: A Case Study with Discussion." In C. Wankel (ed.), *Teaching Arts and Sciences with the New Social Media: Cutting-Edge Technologies in Higher Education* (vol. 3). Bingley, U.K.: Emerald Group, 2011.

Jones, J. B. "The Creepy Treehouse Problem." *Chronicle of Higher Education*, March 9, 2010. Retrieved from http://chronicle.com/blogs/profhacker/the-creepy-treehouse -problem/23027

Junco, R. "Twitter to Improve College Student Engagement." Paper presented at SXSW Interactive, Austin, Texas, 2011.

Junco, R., Heiberger, G., and Loken, E. "The Effect of Twitter on College Student Engagement and Grades." *Journal of Computer Assisted Learning*, 2010, 27(2), 119–132.

Karl, K., and Peluchette, J. " 'Friending' Professors, Parents, and Bosses: A Facebook Connection Conundrum." *Journal of Education for Business*, 2011, 86(4), 213–222.

Kupetz, A. H. "Social Media for the MBA Professor: A Strategy for Increasing Teacher– Student Communication and Tactics for Implementation." In C. Wankel (ed.), *Cutting-Edge Social Media Approaches to Business Education: Teaching with LinkedIn, Facebook, Twitter, Second Life, and Blogs*. Bingley, U.K.: Emerald Group, 2010.

Lampe, C., Ellison, N. B., and Steinfield, C. "Change in Use and Perception of Facebook." Paper presented at the Association for Computing Machinery conference on computer-supported cooperative work, New York, 2008, pp. 721–730.

Lenhart, A., Ling, R., Campbell, S., and Purcell, K. "Teens and Mobile Phones," 2010. Retrieved from http://pewinternet.org/Reports/2010/Teens-and-Mobile-Phones /Chapter-3/Sleeping-with-the-phone-on-or-near-the-bed.aspx

Lenhart, A., Purcell, K., Smith, A., and Zickuhr, K. "Social Media and Mobile Internet Use among Teens and Young Adults," April 20, 2010. Retrieved from the Pew Internet and American Life Project Web site http://pewinternet.org/Reports/2010/Social -Media-and-Young-Adults.aspx

Locke, M. "Six Spaces of Social Media," 2007. Retrieved from TEST http://test.org .uk/2007/08/10/six-spaces-of-social-media/

Madge, C., Meek, J., Wellens, J., and Hooley, T. "Facebook, Social Integration and Informal Learning at University: It Is More for Socializing and Talking to Friends About Work than for Actually Doing Work." *Learning Media, and Technology*, 2009, 34(2), 141–155.

Malesky, L. A., and Peters, C. "Defining Appropriate Professional Behavior for Faculty and University Students on Social Networking Websites." *Higher Education*, 2011, 61. doi:10.1007/s10734–011–9451-x

Maranto, G., and Barto, M. "Paradox and Promise: MySpace, Facebook and the Sociopolitics of Social Networking in the Writing Classroom." *Computers and Compositions*, 2009, 27(1), 36–47.

Mazer, J. P., Murphy, R. E., and Simonds, C. J. "I'll See You on '*Facebook*': The Effects of Computer-Mediated Teacher Self-Disclosure on Student Motivation, Affective Learning, and Classroom Climate." *Communication Education*, 2007, 56(1), 1–17.

Mazer, J. P., Murphy, R. E., and Simonds, C. "The Effects of Teacher Self-Disclosure via Facebook on Teacher Credibility." *Learning, Media, and Technology*, 2009, 34(2), 175–183.

McBride, M. C., and Wahl, S. T. "To Say or Not to Say? Teachers' Management of Privacy Boundaries in the Classroom." *Texas Speech Communication Journal*, 2005, 30(1), 8–22.

McEwan, B. "Compressed Crystals: A Metaphor for Computer-Mediated Identity Performances." Paper presented at the National Communication Association Conference, New Orleans, 2011.

McLoughlin, C., and Lee, M. J. W. "Social Software and Participatory Learning: Pedagogical Choices with Technology Affordances in the Web 2.0 Era." Paper presented at Ascilite conference in Singapore, 2007. Retrieved from www.ascilite.org.au /conferences/singapore07/procs/mcloughlin.pdf

Mehrabian, A. "Significance of Posture and Position in the Communication of Attitude and Status Relationships." *Psychological Bulletin*, 1969, 71(5), 359–372.

Mendez, J. P., and others. "To Friend or Not to Friend: Academic Interaction on Facebook." *International Journal of Instructional Technology and Distance Learning*, 2009, 6(9). Retrieved from http://itdl.org/Journal/Sep_09/article03.htm

Moran, M., Seaman, J., and Tinti-Kane, H. *Teaching, Learning, and Sharing: How Today's Higher Education Faculty Use Social Media*. Boston: Pearson Learning Solutions and Babson Survey Research Group, 2011.

Ophus, J. D., and Abbitt, J. T. "Exploring the Potential Perceptions of Social Networking Systems in University Courses." *Journal of Online Learning and Teaching*, 2009, 5(4), 639–648.

Oradini, F., and Saunders, G. "The Use of Social Networking by Students and Staff in Higher Education." Paper presented at the iLearning Forum, European Institute of E-Learning, Paris, France, 2008. Retrieved from http://www.eife-l.org/publications/proceedings/ilf08/contributions/improving-quality-of-learning-withtechnologies/

Ossiansson, E. "Facebook 'Friendship' as Educational Practice." In C. Wankel (ed.), *Cutting-Edge Social Media Approaches to Business Education: Teaching with LinkedIn, Facebook, Twitter, Second Life, and Blogs*. Bingley, U.K.: Emerald Group, 2010.

O'Sullivan, P. B. "Masspersonal Communication: Rethinking the Mass-Interpersonal Divide." Paper presented at a meeting of the International Communication Association, New York, 2005.

Owen, P. R., and Zwahr-Castro, J. "Boundary Issues in Academia: Student Perceptions of Student Boundary Crossings." *Ethics and Behavior*, 2007, 17(2), 117–129.

Pascarella, E., and Terenzini, P. How College Affects Students: Findings and Insights from Twenty Years of Research. San Francisco: Jossey-Bass, 1991.

Petronio, S. S. *Boundaries of Privacy*. Albany: State University of New York, 2002.

Plax, T. G., Kearney, P., McCroskey, J. C., and Richmond, V. P. "Power in the Classroom VI: Verbal Control Strategies, Nonverbal Immediacy, and Affective Learning." *Communication Education*, 1986, 35(2), 43–55.

Roblyer, M. D., and others. "Findings on Facebook in Higher Education: A Comparison of College Faculty and Student Uses and Perceptions of Social Networking Sites." *Internet and Higher Education*, 2010, 13(3), 134–140.

Schirmer, J. "Fostering Meaning and Community in Writing Course via Social Media." In C. Wankel (ed.), *Teaching Arts and Sciences with the New Social Media: Cutting-Edge Technologies in Higher Education* (vol. 3). Bingley, U.K.: Emerald Group, 2011.

Schroeder, A., Minocha, S., and Schneider, C. "The Strengths, Weaknesses, Opportunities, and Threats of Using Social Software in Higher and Further Education Teaching and Learning. *Journal of Computer Assisted Learning*, 2010, 26(3), 159–174.

Schwartz, H. L. "Facebook: The New Classroom Commons?" *Chronicle of Higher Education*, September 28, 2009. Retrieved from http://chronicle.com/article/Facebook-The-New-Classroom/48575/

Selwyn, N. "'Screw Blackboard ... Do It on Facebook!': An Investigation of Students' Educational Use of Facebook." Paper presented at Poke 1.0, Facebook Social Research Symposium, London, 2007. Retrieved from http://www.lse.ac.uk/collections/informationSystems/newsAndEvents/2008events/selwynpaper.pdf

Smith, A., Rainie, L., and Zickuhr, K. "College Students and Technology," [2011]. Retrieved from the Pew Internet and American Life Project Web site, pewinternet.org/Reports/2011/College-students-and-technology/Report.aspx

Stein, J. "Defining Creepy Treehouses," 2008. Retrieved from http://flexknowlogy.learningfield.org/2008/04/09/defining-creepy-tree-house/

Sturgeon, C. M., and Walker, C. "Faculty on Facebook: Confirm or Deny." Paper presented at the fourteenth Annual Instructional Technology Conference, Murfreesboro, Tennessee, 2009.

Subrahmanyam, K., Reich, S. M., Waechter, N., and Espinoza, G. "Online and Offline Social Networks. Use of Social Networking Sites by Emerging Adults." *Journal of Applied Developmental Psychology*, 2008, *29*(6), 420–433.

Thompson, B. "How College Freshmen Communicate Student Academic Support: A Grounded Theory Study." *Communication Education*, 2008, *57*(1), 123–144.

Wesch, M. (n.d.). http://mediatedcultures.net/youtube.htm

Woodward, S., Jones, S., and Blackey, H. "Facebook: Social or Learning Communities." Paper presented at the fifth International Blended Learning Conference, Hatfield, U.K, 2010. Retrieved from http://www.herts.ac.uk/fms/documents/teaching-and-learning/blu/conference2010/proceedings-of-the-fifth-international-blended-learning-conference-held-on-16–17-june-2010.pdf#page=76

BREE MCEWAN *is an assistant professor in the Department of Communication at Western Illinois University.*

3

This chapter explores differences in generational values and behaviors. Understanding these differences will help faculty members set interpersonal boundaries that create an environment in which both student and teacher feel respected, appreciated, and capable.

Millennial Values and Boundaries in the Classroom

Chip Espinoza

One does not have to spend much time in a department meeting or faculty lounge to get a feel for the bewilderment many educators are experiencing in the classroom today. Conversations of plagiarism and grade inflation have given way to stories of parental interference, students' unrealistic expectations, and a perceived indifference to authority as it relates to the position or experience of another. For example, I recently had a student ask me, "What qualifies you to be teaching me?" Not long ago I was presenting at a conference in India, and a professor shared her experience of a student asking her "What could you possibly teach me that I can't find on the Internet?"

Students' relationships with authority and information are changing rapidly, and this presents a new set of interpersonal boundary challenges for us as faculty. The topic of setting boundaries often conjures up thoughts of how to protect oneself. The intent of this chapter is to explore how good rapport between teacher and student can be developed and in turn create an engaging learning environment that promotes self-giving rather than self-protecting behaviors. In their book *Academically Adrift: Limited Learning on College Campuses*, Arum and Roska (2011) claim that today's students are underperforming due to a lack of preparation, academic rigor, and individual study time and too much nonacademic activity. Their findings also suggest that declining student performance is due partly to the changing culture of the academy—a culture that encourages educators to shift from a focus on students to a focus both on relationships with other

NEW DIRECTIONS FOR TEACHING AND LEARNING, no. 131, Fall 2012 © Wiley Periodicals, Inc.
Published online in Wiley Online Library (wileyonlinelibrary.com) • DOI: 10.1002/tl.20025

faculty and on publishing for professional survival. Arum and Roska refer to the shift as self-protecting behavior and a *disengagement compact*: "I'll leave you alone if you leave me alone" (Kuh's, 2003, p. 28). I suggest that distancing oneself from students can lead to student disengagement.

Connecting with students does not have to be at the expense of academic rigor. Rigor and relationship are not antithetical. This chapter explores generational differences and the Millennial generation in particular and then provides strategies for clarifying, maintaining, and at times adjusting boundaries with Millennial students. We explore Millennial (also known as Gen Y) students' ideals and the resulting implications for educators, vis-à-vis classroom management, use of technology, and student expectations. We also briefly examine the theory of how age cohorts are formed, the notion of cohort effect, and the skills needed to thrive in today's classroom.

Generational differences can significantly affect the day-to-day life of faculty. Spending a semester with a group of people you don't "get" and who don't "get" you can both demotivate and deenergize even the most dedicated faculty members. A colleague told me, "I have had a class every once in a while that I just didn't click with but it seems that I have strung several semesters together recently." And just when you think you have one cohort of students figured out, a new generation arrives on the scene, leaving you with the challenge of understanding how *they* think and act.

Arguably, the ability to relate to students is a critical aspect of teaching and will only continue to grow in importance. There are some faculty members who believe that the student must adapt to the teacher. I would like for us to suspend that notion and consider that it is the people with the most responsibility who have to adapt first. This does not mean that students do not need to mature or change, and it does not mean that faculty members must give in to the wants and preferences of a generation that holds a different set of values. However, it does mean that it is incumbent on educators to do the adaptive work necessary to be effective in the classroom. Ironically, it is often our own experience that can become a barrier to our ability to adapt. One example is the "sage on the stage" mentality.

Sage on the Stage

The challenge of knowledge transfer between generations is not a new phenomenon. Via hieroglyphics, the oral tradition, or print, generations have always *downloaded* their wisdom. Perhaps the first revolutionary disruption in the learning experience was sparked by the printing press. It could be debated that Johannes Gutenberg presented the first real challenge to the teacher as sole authority or meaning maker for students. The printed word introduced myriad different voices and allowed students to access multiple influences.

Alison King (1993) warned that the twenty-first century would require a different model of teaching. "In contrast to the transmittal model illustrated by the classroom lecture-note-taking scenario, the constructivist model places students at the center of the process—actively participating in thinking and discussing ideas while making meaning for themselves. And the professor, instead of being the *sage on the stage*, functions as *a guide on the side*" (p. 30). Not since the printing press has there been a greater disruptive technology to teaching than the Internet.

King was asking us to suspend the bias of "how we were taught" or "how we learned to teach" and instead consider the need to adapt to the times for the sake of the student. I suggest we are already beyond *guide on the side* and our role today is that of colearner—we are learning *with*.

Relationships Redefined

Thanks to the Internet and accessibility, today's students are the first generation that has not needed an authority figure to access information. Unlike prior generations, Millennials do not have a *felt need* to build a relationship with authority figures. Conversely, there is a generation of teachers waiting to be revered in the same way they once admired their professors. It is a perfect kind of storm and warrants significant consideration. We have a generation of students who do not feel the need to initiate a relationship with authority figures and a generation of teachers who may not know how or do not consider it their responsibility to build a relationship with students. It is a *generational thing*.

One effect of technology is that Millennials will exhaust themselves looking for information electronically before they will seek out and ask an authority figure. Espinoza, Ukleja, and Rusch (2010) quote Cameron Johnson, a Millennial entrepreneur: " 'I don't know' is not in my generation's vocabulary because it is only a search away" (p. 5). It is not that Millennials do not value the teacher's experience or knowledge; they are just wired to look elsewhere first. Many teachers interpret such behavior as a minimizing of their role or as a lack of respect. Couple that perception with seeing a student in your class smiling while gazing into a laptop and you have a recipe for an emotional hijack.

Generational Perspective

Contemporary society readily, if not naturally, accepts the notion of a generation as a form of differentiation or comparison (that is, "My generation didn't ask questions; we just did what we were told to do"). The idea of a generation is not new and can be found throughout ancient literature. Originally, the concept had biological roots in family, where the term *generation* refers to kinship or successive parent–child relationships

(Biggs, 2007). However, there are also psychological and sociological dimensions in the sense of belonging and identity that can define a generation (Mannheim, [1928] 1952; Ryder, 1965). The psychosocial view of a generation is also referred to as an *age cohort*. The latter theory of a generation emerged in an essay written by German sociologist Karl Mannheim ([1928] 1952).

Mannheim's essay is titled "The Problem of Generations." Mannheim's work is revered as the most systematic and fully developed treatment of generation through a sociological lens (Pilcher, 1994). Gilleard and Higgs (2002) write: "Mannheim sought to describe three elements making up a generation: a shared temporal location (*i.e.* generational site or birth cohort), shared historical location (*i.e.* generation as actuality—exposure to a common period or era), and finally a shared socio-cultural location (*i.e.* generational consciousness—or 'entelechy')" (p. 373). Simply put, a generation is defined as an identifiable group that shares birth years, age location, and significant life events at critical developmental stages.

Student Ideals and Expectations

Every generation of students has been shaped by a number of powerful influences including parental involvement, sociopolitical events, policy making, and technology. The results of such influences are referred to as *cohort effects*. The idea is that people experiencing a sociological context at a similar age may forge a perspective or mind-set that stays with them as they grow up and grow old (Settersten and Mayer, 1997). As an example, today's traditional students have had a tremendous amount of attention, praise, help, and expectation showered on them. They expect the same in the classroom. Millennials are confused when they encounter people they perceive to be not "for them"; these students expect people to do everything possible to make them successful.

One boundary that has definitely become more sentient is parental involvement, or what some may refer to as interference. It is not uncommon for parents to petition teachers to change grades or excuse absences for their child. Whether students live at home or on their own, they are still very connected to their parents. They feel collectively special in the eyes of their parents and their community.

Underlying Values in the Classroom

Values drive attitudes and behaviors. Wherever there are competing values, there is opportunity for confusion and discord, and the classroom is no exception. The primary challenge that we face when working with today's students is suspending the bias of our own experiences. Doing so allows us to ask such questions as "Why does their behavior bother me?" or "What adaptations must I make to be effective in my role?" A powerful framework for suspending bias can be found in Bandler and Grinder's (1975) work in neurolinguistic programming (NLP). In their book *NLP for Teachers*, Churches and Terry reveal a core tenet of NLP: "We cannot change anyone else's behavior, we can only change our own" (2007, p. 5). NLP provides a useful framework for exploring the relational space between teachers and students. NLP asks that we look at situations or encounters through three lenses. The first lens is how we experience the situation (feelings, emotions, thoughts, and so on). The second lens is the perspective of the student (to the degree we can imagine it) and how he or she is experiencing the situation. The third lens is "going to 30,000 feet" and taking on the role of looking down on the scenario as an objective observer.

Before we put on the second lens, I would like to point out some differences in the teacher's perspective that can make or break *generational rapport*. The difference between connecting effectively with students in the classroom or not connecting has more to do with how we respond to our students than with our perceptions of them. Table 3.1 is a good tool for reflection.

Once you have suspended the bias of your own experience and reflected on your own perspective, it is helpful to explore student expectations. While doing research for our book on managing Millennials, my colleagues and I identified several intrinsic values held by the Millennial generation, values that drive behavior that we perceived as distinctly

Table 3.1. Effective and Challenged Perspectives

	Effective Perspective	*Challenged Perspective*
Adaptability	Explore your own need to change in order to teach in the current context	Talk about how students need to change or grow up
Self-efficacy	Believe there is something you can do about your situation	Believe that there is little you can do about your situation
Confidence	Allow your students to challenge you (ideas and processes)	Sanction or punish your students for challenging you
Power	Use the power of relationship versus the power of your position	Rely strictly on your positional authority
Energy	Let the students make you feel young	Let the students make you feel old
Success	See yourself as key to your students' success	See students as an impediment to your own success

Source: Adapted from Espinoza, Ukleja, and Rusch (2010).

different from values of previous generations and values that influence interpersonal boundaries. In the next section, I review Millennial generation values and related expectations and suggest strategies for dealing with them in the context of interpersonal boundaries. When you understand (not necessarily agree with) what students expect, you can more effectively negotiate and set interpersonal boundaries.

Reward: Students Expect Guarantees. A marked difference I noticed between my students in the early 1990s and mid-2000s could be seen on the first day of each semester. Today's students actually read the syllabus. They love to go line by line with a red pen. It is not uncommon to hear questions like "It says twelve- to fifteen-page midterm paper due the last class before spring break. Is fifteen pages an A and twelve pages a C?" Students have their sights set on the highest possible grade and often confuse quantity of work with quality of work. Any reward that is less than expected triggers expectation hangover. Many people have referred to today's students as the "trophy generation," alluding to the fact that they received a trophy just for showing up in youth activities. Millennials are about meeting expectations, so being clear about expectations is critically important. If your expectations are listed in terms of units (numbers of pages, length of time, amount of references, and so on) and they comply, they expect full credit for their work regardless of the quality. They want a guarantee for the quantity of work they do. More poignantly, they feel entitled.

I have several colleagues who get frustrated when students ask for a study guide because they think students want things to be made easier for them. I disagree. Students primarily desire study guides because of their preoccupation with wanting to know what is expected of them, not to make life easier. As you will read later, I agree that students value simplicity, but when they ask for study help, it is because they want to know what *you* expect them to know. You can be sure they will be rigorous when it comes to using study guides.

Students today are savvy consumers and often consider their educational experience to be simply a service for which they pay. When students question the grade they receive or assignments they have been given, I find it is a perfect opportunity to discuss expectations (both theirs and mine). I know this won't work in some contexts due to class size, but I have a colleague who asks students to write out what they thought was unfair about the grade (time, preparation, topic, and the like) and what they could have done to score better. She uses the "unfair" comments to improve her preparation and uses them as a means for coaching, recommending resources, and demonstrating expectations.

Strategy Summary. Prepare to clearly define your expectations. Be open to discussing your expectations, and be ready to adhere to them. Students often perceive the grades they receive as indicators of their relationship with you rather than with their academic performance. The boundary challenge is to separate your self from your role when students take a grade personally or challenge how well they think they have been prepared for a test. If you don't self-differentiate, it is easy to get defensive and contribute to escalating tension.

Self-Expression: Students Expect to Have a Say. Students want to express themselves. Although generations may have grown up under the idiom "Children should be seen and not heard," today's students have been given a voice. Savvy marketers realize that parents consult with their children even on major purchases, such as automobiles, technology, and vacations. Young people are used to being listened to. If you want to truly engage them, you must solicit and embrace their voice. There are two aspects about voice that I think are important to understand.

The first aspect is soliciting their voice in the classroom. One thing I learned through my research that had an immediate impact on my teaching was how to stimulate a discussion. As I reflect, my approach to class discussion was very "sage on the stage"—I, as the professor, figure out what is important to me, and we will talk about it. Students want to participate in dialogue, but due to their desire to achieve or be right, they are leery of questions such as "What did you like about the article?" If I started with such a question, the only sound I would hear is the humming of the lights or nervous movement. Students love to problem-solve and prefer to critique rather than be critiqued. Therefore, I started discussions with questions such as "What did you not like about the article?" or "What improvements would you make to the concept?" Ironically, that little shift set the classroom abuzz with discussion.

The second aspect of encouraging their voice is allowing students the opportunity to express how they are experiencing your class. Why wait for the end-of-semester evaluations? Students thrive when they are invited to make a contribution, problem-solve, or brainstorm. I am not suggesting that you have to implement every suggestion or that you acquiesce to their every need; however, encouraging them to provide feedback is likely to deepen their engagement in the class and may also provide both them and you with important points of reflection.

Strategy Summary. Prepare to tap into the students' voices frequently and listen to what they like and dislike about assignments, you, or the class. Expect students to offer feedback. Don't be offended. The students are exercising their voice and trying to help.

Attention: Students Expect a Quick Response. Students are accustomed to getting attention and expect you to be there for them when they need help. Students see school life, work life, and social life as one. They will do work at school, school at work, social life at school and work. Technology has allowed them to be untethered with real-time access to many dimensions of life. While the generation before them (Gen X) is noted for desiring work–life balance, today's students do not see the two in conflict. They blend both seamlessly. Technology has allowed them to

NEW DIRECTIONS FOR TEACHING AND LEARNING • DOI: 10.1002/tl

access work and play in real time simultaneously. Unfortunately, they think everyone works the way they do. I had a student e-mail me a paper for which I had given her a one-week extension. It was time-stamped Monday, 1:02AM PDT. She stuck her head in my office on Monday morning around 8:30 and asked me what I thought about her paper. She was a little frustrated that I had not yet read it.

Time is perhaps one of the most immovable boundaries, and yet Millennials still seem to expect it to bend for them. Technology has not only allowed them to be plugged in from anywhere, but it has also conditioned them to expect to have their needs met *now*. Video on demand, instant money transfers from the mother ship, and self-checkout terminals are just a few of the conveniences that they have known practically their whole lives. Communication is just another aspect of their life that is *now*.

I would not argue that technology has caused us to be better communicators, but it has transformed how and when we converse. At the beginning of each course, solicit your students' expectations regarding communication, including communication tools and response time, and clarify for them what you are willing to do. Do they expect you to respond in the evening and on weekends and holidays? What is an appropriate response time? There is not a right or wrong set of boundaries regarding communications; rather, the key is to clarify expectations and create a clear understanding that takes into account the students' wishes and your own work style and sense of privacy.

Strategy Summary. Prepare to get texts and e-mails at all times and for students to expect that you will respond immediately. Students see your availability as twenty-four hours a day, seven days a week. Be clear about how and when you will communicate. You may find it helpful to let your students talk about preferred modes and times of communication with you. There may be a situation in which you find the students' expectations unreasonable; that is okay. It is important for them to have their say but not necessarily their way. Our students appreciate being invited into the discussion.

Achievement: Students Expect Affirmation. Students are not only accustomed to people being attentive to them, but they also expect positive attention. Anything short of affirmation is disconcerting to these students. This is problematic because one of the primary roles of a teacher is that of evaluator and constructive critic. Students who believe they are not achieving are likely to become defensive. We must try not to take personally students' defensiveness or projections. The good news is that many of these students really do want to achieve. If we can resist getting hooked by their response to negative feedback, we can help them identify areas for improvement.

Another element of understanding Millennials and feedback is that they are unnerved by formality. Asking a student to meet in your office after class is likely to raise the student's anxiety level and perhaps close him or her off to your feedback. The more informal you can make a conversation, the better. It can also be helpful to use yourself as an example, making it clear that you also faced challenges: "I struggled with the same thing as a student." Perhaps the most important thing is to let students know that you believe in their ability. In essence, by expressing support, you are better able to disarm student defensiveness and get to a place of communication.

Strategy Summary. Prepare to be blamed for the student's performance (for example, the test was too tough or the student was not adequately prepared by you) and to get a call from a concerned parent. Don't take it personally. Try, whenever possible, to create informal contexts for feedback and to express support while also critiquing the student's work.

Informality: Students Expect You to Be Friendly. Students see titles and formal authority as inauthentic and a barrier to building real relationships. For the most part, the generation was raised by Baby Boomer parents who valued being friends with their children. It is natural for a student to expect a similar friendship with teachers. In addition, today's students live their lives in public and have no problem with self-disclosure. On a personal level, I could never imagine having conversations with my parents that my children have had with me. Just as young people are less formal and more self-disclosing with their parents, they may relate to teachers in much the same manner.

Social networks raise significant boundary questions for educators, many of whom struggle with whether to connect with students on social media sites. My advice is to be clear about your own comfort level and competency with social media and to also articulate your social media boundaries so that students know what to expect. (For additional consideration of boundaries and social media, see Chapter Two of this sourcebook.) The boundary questions we face today on social media are an extension of boundary questions we faced previously with students. Whether it is via Facebook, e-mail, text, or getting a cup of coffee on campus with a student, be aware that Millennial students prefer to approach professors as friends. Although students will approach you as a friend, it is not their expectation that you will be friends for life or that you will have a relationship beyond their matriculation. They just feel more comfortable with an informal approach to relating.

Strategy Summary. Prepare to be addressed informally, quizzed about your personal life, and invited into the student's world. Understand that from the student's perspective, this is not inappropriate; seek to balance this with boundaries that feel ethical and appropriate for you as an educator. Whatever your boundary, make sure it is consistent.

Simplicity: Students Expect Everything to Be Negotiable. Students will work extremely hard at trying to make something easier, course requirements in particular. I return to the example of my students red-penning the syllabus: What if I turn the paper in after spring break? When do you plan on doing the grading? By the way, two fifteen-page papers is too much work for a 300-level class, the quizzes are weighted too heavily, and the reading assigned is excessive." They will take the practice beyond identifying your expectations to evaluating whether the workload is unfair or unrealistic from their perspective.

As I stated earlier, our students have grown up having a voice in their families. That is not a bad thing. They got to vote on where they vacationed, where they lived, and, in some cases, where they went to school. They are refreshing in that if you ask them what they think, they will actually tell you. People who are effective at relating with Millennials do not mind negotiating with them and view it as an energizing engagement.

I decided to try the concept out in one of my classes. I had assigned two texts. One book was a typical scholarly text and the other was a practitioner text, *Pour Your Heart Into It*, Howard Schultz's accounting of how Starbucks grew to be a household name. I decided to institute a weekly twenty-question quiz on the Starbucks book. The students were allowed to challenge any answer on the quiz but had to give a compelling argument for their disagreement. It was not long before I realized the students were reading for comprehension cover to cover. They loved the opportunity to challenge. It gave them voice and played into their desire to be participative in the learning experience. There was no question that I was the final authority as teacher, but I found that a relationship based on learning *with* the students rather than on our conventional roles proved effective as a motivator for students. And the practice of rejecting some of the students' challenges helped me grow professionally. My relationship with students in the classroom is important to me, and I know there have been times when my inability to say no (accepting late assignments, excusing absences, and the like) may have hurt them down the road. Ironically, I found the quiz practice helpful for being able to say no to students. There are some situations that are nonnegotiable, and that is appropriate.

Strategy Summary. Prepare to negotiate assignments and deadlines— not as a "giving in" posture but as an engaging one. Do not be offended that students are better at commenting on what they don't like than on what they do like. Be clear regarding what is nonnegotiable for you.

Multitasking: Students Expect You to Know They Can Do Several Things at Once. Students believe they can do several things at once due to their proficiency with technology. This shows up particularly when you are lecturing. This drives the sage on the stage crazy. As a teacher, there are few things that frustrate me more than someone who doesn't seem to notice that I am lecturing. So, I decided to set boundaries for the use of technology in class. I tell the students that when their use of technology becomes a distraction to other students, they must turn it off. If it is only a distraction to them, they must be prepared for the consequences (such as missing important information, assignments).

One night I was two-thirds through a three-hour class and noticed a student that had been preoccupied with her laptop screen all night. The two colleagues beside her were also looking intently at her computer. I just couldn't resist positioning myself to see what they were enthralled about. It was a large amphitheater-style classroom so it took me a while but I eventually worked my way into a spot to see what was so alluring. She was video streaming the lecture to a friend in her dorm who was sick. I am so glad that I did not draw negative attention to her. I learned a great lesson that day: many times students are using their technology as a learning tool rather than trying to ignore me.

Strategy Summary. Don't get triggered by students' apparent inattentiveness. Don't hesitate to set boundaries for the use of technology.

Meaning: Students Expect You to Explain the Why. Students want to know "why." It is not a defiant "why" but rather a desire to find meaning in an assignment or requirement. "Why is this important for me to learn?" Some of the best teaching opportunities are when you encounter the "why." I taught an organizational behavior class in which I gave an option to the class to participate as teams or individuals. The syllabus stated that if the class decided on a team structure, each member of the team would be awarded the same grade. The syllabus allowed for an individual to petition for a different grade to be awarded, but the student had to meet with his or her triad and critique the two other team members' involvement and make an argument for being assigned a higher grade. Every class opted for the team approach. It was always smooth sailing until midterms. In one particular class, a potential magna cum laude student saw her perfect GPA slipping away because of her team's performance. She took every opportunity to voice to me her dissatisfaction with her colleagues, but by the end of the semester, her frustration was solely focused on me. She lamented, "I have worked so hard and you have ruined my GPA and life with this stupid class." I reminded her of the option in the syllabus, but she insisted that she didn't want to be the bad guy—she said that was my job as the professor. She eventually opted to confront her team. They agreed with her assessment of their participation. She received her A, her gold cord, and a great offer from a top-three accounting firm. She stopped by my office before leaving the campus and asked me why I designed the class that way. I explained that organizational behavior was not about an individual's performance but about a collective performance. I told her that I never doubted her academic ability, but I worried that she would be rendered ineffective for overfunctioning and not having the ability to hold others accountable for their performance.

A few years later, she contacted me. She told me that it took her a long time to get over being mad at me, but the greatest lesson she remembered from college was being able to confront underperforming team members.

Strategy Summary. Prepare to connect the dots for students and do not be put off by their "whys." When students understand the why, they are more likely to work hard and appreciate your investment in them.

Conclusion

I would like to close this chapter by reiterating the importance of viewing teaching as a personal growth opportunity. No matter how frustrated or even puzzled we become, we can look for opportunities to enhance our classroom management and teaching skills. It is easy to find ways that our students can grow or act differently, but we must also try to keep focused on what we can do differently.

Unfortunately, I have encountered many educators who have an external locus of control. They view the Millennial challenge as something that happened to them and believe they are powerless to do anything about it. They believe themselves to be victims of circumstance. It isn't that they do not want to be good teachers, they just do not know where to start or what to do. In essence, they are stuck. Stuck people experience the regression of the imagination and cannot think anything could ever be any different from their current situation. The willingness to adapt, however, demonstrates an internal locus of control. That is to say, you believe there is something you can do about your dilemma or frustration—you are not stuck. Consequently, making adaptations leads to greater optimism about your future and the potential of your students.

References

Arum, R., and Roska, J. *Academically Adrift: Limited Learning on College Campuses.* Chicago: University of Chicago Press, 2011.

Bandler, R., and Grinder, J. *Patterns of the Hypnotic Techniques of Milton H. Erickson, M.D.* Cupertino, Calif.: Meta Publications, 1975.

Biggs, S. "Thinking about Generations: Conceptual Positions and Policy Implications." *Journal of Social Issues,* 2007, 63(4), 695–711.

Churches, R., and Terry, R. *NLP for Teachers: How to Be a Highly Effective Teacher.* Bethel, Conn.: Crown House, 2007.

Espinoza, C., Ukleja, M., and Rusch, C. *Managing the Millennials Discover the Core Competencies for Managing Today's Workforce.* Hoboken, N.J.: John Wiley & Sons, 2010.

Gilleard, C., and Higgs, P. "The Third Age: Class, Cohort or Generation?" *Ageing and Society,* 2002, 22(3), 369–382. doi:10.1017/S0144686X0200870X

King, A. "From Sage on the Stage to Guide on the Side." *College Teaching,* 1993, 41(1), 30.

Kuh, G. "What We Are Learning About Student Engagement." *Change,* 2003, 35(2), 24–32.

Mannheim, K. *Essays on the Sociology of Knowledge.* New York: Oxford University Press, 1952. (Originally published 1928.)

Pilcher, J. "Mannheim's Sociology of Generations: An Undervalued Legacy." *British Journal of Sociology,* 1994, 45(3), 481–494.

Ryder, N. B. "The Cohort as a Concept in the Study of Social Change." *American Sociological Review*, 1965, *30*(6), 843–861.

Schultz, H., and Yang, D. J. *Pour Your Heart Into It: How Starbucks Built a Company One Cup at a Time* (1st ed.). New York: Hyperion, 1997.

Settersten, R. A., and Mayer, K. U. "The Measurement of Age, Age Structuring, and the Life Course." *Annual Review of Sociology*, 1997, *23*, 233.

CHIP ESPINOZA is a coauthor of Managing the Millennials: Discover the Core Competencies for Managing Today's Workforce *(2010) and an adjunct professor at Concordia University.*

4

Working with adult learners presents a unique set of interpersonal boundary questions. This chapter considers characteristics of adult learners, relevant frameworks for considering boundaries, and four specific strategies to help instructors increase clarity and intention regarding boundaries with adult students.

We're All Adults Here: Clarifying and Maintaining Boundaries with Adult Learners

Melanie Booth, Harriet L. Schwartz

Carrie is a thirty-seven-year old married mother of two school-age children. She manages a paralegal department in a large corporate law firm and has fifteen years of professional experience. She also takes care of her aging father and volunteers at her children's elementary school. She has returned to an adult-serving university to complete her bachelor's degree to increase her employability. Like Carrie, Jonathan, a forty-five-year old single father of three kids, has a full-time job: he is an information technology specialist and is enrolled in an MBA program designed for working professionals. His educational goal is linked to his professional goal in that he hopes to start his own technology consulting firm. Both Carrie and Jonathan are adult learners in higher education as defined by the Council for Adult and Experiential Learning: they are students "who have assumed major life responsibilities and commitments, such as work, family, and community activities" (Flint and Associates, 1999, p. ix).

Prior to the 1970s, information about adults as learners was based on psychological perspectives about learning in general (Merriam and Caffarella, 1999); however, with the publications of several key texts, the most notable being Malcolm Knowles's *The Adult Learner: A Neglected Species* (1973), theorists and practitioners began to focus on attempting to understand the unique learning processes and characteristics of adults as learners. Knowles's influential work described the process of andragogy to

NEW DIRECTIONS FOR TEACHING AND LEARNING, no. 131, Fall 2012 © Wiley Periodicals, Inc.
Published online in Wiley Online Library (wileyonlinelibrary.com) • DOI: 10.1002/tl.20026

include elements designed to establish a suitable physical and psychological climate for adults as learners, including mutual respect, collaboration, supportiveness, openness, and fun. Andragogy also calls for educators to involve adult learners in the planning and assessment of their own learning (Knowles and Associates, 1984). Andragogy has since shaped how many adult educators approach their teaching practice as well as their relationships with students. However, andragogy and other more recent theories of adult learning and development have not yet adequately grappled with boundary questions that surface for instructors and their adult students.

In this chapter, we discuss the characteristics of working with adult learners that have led us to explore questions about boundaries between us and our students. We then identify how we might define, set, maintain, adjust, and work close to interpersonal boundaries with adult students through our consideration of two frameworks: a relational approach (Jordan, 1991, 2010; Miller and Stiver, 1997; Daloz, 1999) to teaching and learning, and Tom's (1997) deliberate relationship model. We conclude by identifying four specific strategies for effectively and deliberately navigating boundaries with our adult learners. Our focus in this chapter is on creating and maintaining healthy, ethical interpersonal relationships that support our adult students' learning and development. We focus on professional academic relationships between instructors and adult students and explore strategies for subtly and intentionally working close to or modifying boundaries to foster the best conditions for support, motivation, and learning for our adult students and ourselves.

What Is Unique About Working with Adult Students as Learners?

Adult learners have several qualities that evoke questions about boundaries in teaching and learning relationships. A few of the key aspects that come into play as we consider our work and relationships with adults as learners include our students' adult lives and realities, our shared experiences and perspectives, our practice of integrating adult learning principles into our classrooms, and the multifaceted and multiple roles we may hold.

In our experience as educators of adults—in an undergraduate liberal arts program and in a professional, applied graduate program—some boundary questions emerge because of the characteristics of our adult students, namely the depth and breadth of their experiences, their family situations (caring for children or parents, for example), their obligations and responsibilities, and their ages. In addition to being similar to our students in many of these ways, we may experience a specific generational connection with our students; for example, we may share memories of notable events, we may like the same music, and our children may be the same age and may even be in the same school. In that instructors often share some personal characteristics with our students, instructors and their adult learners may find similarities in their professional roles and responsibilities as well. Barnett (2008) contended that in an academic setting, graduate students are expected to "gradually become colleagues and peers to faculty" (p. 9). Nakamura and Shernoff (2009) and Daloz (1986) likewise described faculty welcoming students into the professions through mentoring and apprenticeship approaches. Adult students, however, may already be peers to their faculty in some settings and roles (such as in professional or community organizations).

Many instructors who teach adults adhere to andragogical teaching practices that define the role of instructor as a facilitator of learning or, as the adage cleverly reminds us, "guide on the side, not sage on the stage." In other words, instructors of adults often actively encourage their students to see them as colearners and shepherds of the learning community and encourage students to bring their prior experiences, knowledge, and perspectives into course discussions and assignments. Further, specific teaching practices that we employ—such as reflective journaling, dialogue-based learning, and intentionally having students call us by our first names—may push against traditional student–professor boundaries as well. The approaches to learning that instructors of adult students take may very well create unique boundary questions that might otherwise not be raised with more traditional higher educational teaching practices. The multiple and multifaceted roles that instructors of adults may have, in addition to being the instructor of a course, can also raise unique questions about boundaries; roles such as academic adviser, field supervisor, or research director may characterize the nature of our relationships with learners (Barnett, 2008). Within our role as instructor, we typically not only design the curriculum, facilitate the course, and create a community of learners, but we also must evaluate each individual student's performance and learning and thus provide feedback and determine grades. In other words, a lot is a stake in student–teacher relationships.

Although theoretical and empirical literature about adult learning encourages teachers of adults to allow for and even promote increased connections between ourselves and our students and to reduce the power between us, these connections may also create confusion or even conflict for instructors and students. Further, unlike instructors who work with traditional-age undergraduate students, we may operate from the belief that adult students understand the appropriate scope of teaching–learning relationships and bring what may be considered a more mature relational perspective to our classrooms and offices, which may be an incorrect assumption. Questions about the meaning of boundaries between instructors and their adult students thus emerge for us. At what point does sharing information about ourselves, our lives and experiences, with our students move the relationship close to a boundary? At what point does our attempt to connect personally with our students become too personal? At what point does being a colleague, a peer, a colearner with, or a mentor to our adult students become problematic? At what point have we pushed against or even modified a boundary, and how do we ensure that when we do so, it is with intention to support our students' learning?

Relational and Deliberate Teaching–Learning Interactions

Boundaries have been defined as "basic ground rules for the professional relationship" (Barnett, 2008, p. 5), and, as such, they can create "a strong sense of solidity; we use them to both protect and define us" (Wheatley, 2006, p. 30). Although a sense of boundaries can be helpful for both instructors and students, boundaries can also be experienced as barriers to achieving genuine qualities of teacher–learner relationships that would best support adult students' learning and personal and professional development. We propose two frameworks to consider when navigating boundaries between ourselves and our adult learners: taking a relational approach (Jordan, 1991, 2010; Miller and Stiver, 1997; Daloz, 1999) and enacting a deliberate relationship (Tom, 1997). Combined, these two frameworks allow us to consider the qualities of teacher–learner relationships that support learning and development in adults, along with a process by which we can consider our actions within these relationships.

Taking a Relational Approach to Teaching Adult Learners. Taking a relational approach with adult learners—that is, the intentional engaging in a teaching–learning *relationship* with our students—may help illuminate effective boundaries by revealing which aspects of an interpersonal relationship can best support a student's learning and development. Meaningful academic relationships can serve to enhance adult student learning and development as well as energize and enrich us as teachers (Schwartz, 2011; Schwartz and Holloway, 2012). This understanding of meaningful academic relationships is further enriched by relational cultural theory, a human development theory which suggests that we grow and develop in relation with others (Miller and Stiver, 1997; Jordan, 2010). "Growth-fostering relationships are characterized by: (1) an increase in energy; (2) increased knowledge and clarity . . . ; (3) creativity and productivity; (4) a greater sense of worth; and (5) a desire for more connection" (Miller and Stiver, in Jordan, 2010, pp. 3–4).

A sense of authenticity is foundational in relational practice between students and instructors. Daloz (1999) contends that supporting adult learners requires that we genuinely attend to students' whole lives: "Knowing what is important to our students as individuals, we can more readily help them find connections between the lives they live and the subjects we teach" (p. 111). Knowing what is important to our students as individuals requires knowing them *as* individuals—their hopes, fears, experiences, and goals—and also requires that they know us as authentic and real human beings. According to Brookfield (2006), an authentic teacher is "seen as a flesh-and-blood human being with passions, enthusiasm, frailties, and emotions, not someone who hides behind a collection of learned role behaviors appropriate to the title of professor" (p. 5). Brookfield calls this phenomenon "personhood," which aligns with what Tom (1997) has called "presence."

Presence in the teaching framework means being a genuine person in our interactions with students. It begins with sharing those small details that allow our personal lives to show through the professional demeanor, but it is much more profound than that. The most essential element is to make known that real people do the work we do. We get indigestion and stay up all night with our children. We have days of self-confidence and days of doubt. Published articles do not appear magically when we sit down at the computer; we have to work at them. This level of presence and disclosure sends the message to students that *their* indigestion, children, doubts, and difficulties are not fatal flaws.

Our own experience as well as our empirical research with adult learn- ers supports the importance of personhood and presence in our teaching– learning relationships. In Schwartz's study (2009), adult graduate students reported that professors who show their humanity, who bring authenticity to their teaching, create a climate of openness; students find these teachers more approachable in times of both academic stress and intellectual explo- ration. Students reported that deep engagement with professors motivated them to work harder, embrace feedback, take intellectual risks, and aspire to levels of achievement and goals beyond what they previously imagined for themselves (Schwartz, 2011, Schwartz and Holloway, 2012). In Booth's study (2007), self-directed adult undergraduate students reported that open communication with their instructors about themselves as individuals helped them learn the course content and also grow personally and profes- sionally; these students found the most effective learning relationships with instructors who acted as colearners and with whom they could have valu- able personal relationships. To ensure a sense of personhood and presence, to share ourselves appropriately, Daloz (1999) contends that proper care is required so that "the gift of self-disclosure can lead to a valuable deepening of the relationship for both partners" (p. 214).

Although authenticity is the foundation of a relational approach with students, caring is a manifestation of this approach. Caring is a receptive and relational stance from which we support students. Caring and its related quality, empathy, require a clear sense of positionality and boundary as they create, and may even intensify, connections between instructor and student. Particularly in the teaching context, empathy may be assumed to diminish the teacher's effectiveness, as a state of overidentification with the student; however, relational cultural theory provides a more complex understanding of empathy. The empathic teacher or adviser must have flex- ible boundaries to remain open to deeply hearing and emotionally knowing the experience of the student (Jordan, 1991). While maintaining this open- ness, the instructor must also hold a clear sense of self as to not get lost in the student's experience and thus become ineffective. Jordan (1991) states, "In order to empathize, one must have a well-differentiated sense of self in addition to an appreciation of and sensitivity to the differentness as well as sameness of the other" (p. 69).

Adult graduate students in Rossiter's study (1999) identified seven components of caring and empathy: "to be noticed, to be understood, to have one's concerns be a priority for another, to be shown one's best self, to value the one caring, to trust and receive, and to be respected" (pp. 209–210). These same students indicated that they tried to determine the appropriate levels of familiarity and reciprocity in their relationships with professors. They reported that certain elements of the graduate school culture, such as being invited to call their professors by their first names, required them to process or more intentionally seek to understand the boundaries. Indeed, it can be helpful to remind ourselves that students are equally challenged by determining appropriate boundaries, and they likely struggle to balance their needs with what they perceive as typical protocol with their professors. Overall, a relational approach—enacted through personhood, presence, empathy, and care—can help support the learning and personal and professional development of adults and can also serve to help identify and clarify effective boundaries. We acknowledge, however, that even with this approach and thus more clarity about why one would share personal information or express empathy and care with students, there is still a need to justify the specific purposes for pushing against or modifying a boundary.

Enacting a Deliberate Relationship with Adult Learners. Many of the questions about boundaries between ourselves and our adult learners can be effectively navigated through what Tom (1997) describes as the deliberate relationship. In the deliberate relationship, the actions of instructors "are done *on purpose* and *for a purpose*" (pp. 12–13), namely to foster learning. When operating from this framework, instructors engage in a critically reflective moment between the impulse to speak and what we actually do. During this moment—this possibly short but significant "pause between the experience of an impulse and its expression" (p. 12)—Tom proposes that instructors ask "Does it serve the long-term obligations of the relationship?" (p. 12).

Tom contends that the deliberate relationship framework offers a hopeful alternative to two existing responses to questions about teacher–learner relationships and boundaries, what she called distance and denial. The response of distance is typically represented by policies and procedures and is grounded in a stance of distrust of both teacher and student. Although the distance response acknowledges the power dynamic inherent in teaching–learning relationships, it also "increases the privilege associated with powerful positions and does not adequately support students' efforts to grow, to demand change in teaching relationships, and to protect themselves" (Tom, 1997, p. 10). In this case, professors are either reacting

NEW DIRECTIONS FOR TEACHING AND LEARNING • DOI: 10.1002/tl

to their own fear vis-à-vis boundaries or are simply following broad policies rather than focusing on an individual student's learning and development or the context of the relationship.

The influence of andragogical practice in adult learning situations often reveals the other kind of response described by Tom (1997): denying the power and positionality of the instructor. As Tom points out, teachers operating from this framework typically wish to emphasize their students' experience, expertise, and maturity. In other words, we're all adults here, so why worry about boundaries? If we operate from this stance of denying our power and positionality, however, we put students in a vulnerable place, often one that results in more confusion, rather than less, about roles, relationships, and appropriate boundaries (Gardner, Dean, and McKaig, 1989; Buck, Mast, Latta, and Kaftan, 2009). This is where awareness of the types of power we may have as educators of adults, how we use power, and how students perceive our power can be helpful in considering how we think about boundaries because, in fact, "faculty–student relationships by their very nature involve a power differential" (Barnett, 2008, p. 9). As Tom (1997) points out, the deliberate relationship explicitly acknowledges the power difference between instructor and student and insists that the instructor, as the person with the power, has the responsibility to be careful and intentional regarding how the power affects the teaching–learning relationship (p. 14). In other words, we have the responsibility to use our power with explicit care because "attempts to disavow our authority are confusing and inauthentic" (Tom, 1997, p. 12) to our students. If we work from a relational approach as described earlier, authenticity is key.

Cranton (1994) defines three different kinds of power often represented in and by adult educators. The first, positional power, comes with authority and represents control over the punishment and rewards associated with learning; the second type of power, personal power, comes through such qualities as expertise, friendship, loyalty, and charisma; political power, the third type of power, comes through control or influence over important decisions around policies, processes, or programs. What is also necessary to navigating boundaries in a deliberate and authentic relationship, then, is to consider how we might use these different types of power to most appropriately motivate learning in our adult students and to consider how our students perceive our power and our relationships with them. If we are to operate in a deliberate relationship, we must use our power as necessary to support learning and also recognize when "holding power becomes hoarding power" (Tom, 1997, p. 16).

As professors we are qualified to comment on the quality of students' academic work. Our own awareness of the inseparability of our personal and professional lives makes us aware that students' lives may be similarly connected. This knowledge authorizes us to point things out—to encourage students to use their personal passions to fuel their academic work, for example. Because we cannot shrug off the power of the position, we must

NEW DIRECTIONS FOR TEACHING AND LEARNING • DOI: 10.1002/tl

be aware that seemingly casual comments or advice may carry more weight than we intend or desire (Tom, 1997).

With adult learners especially, when we often intentionally create opportunities to deeply understand and connect with our students' educational, personal, and professional history and current contexts, an intentionally appropriate use of power becomes even more critical.

One of the great benefits of Tom's (1997) deliberate relationship framework for considering boundaries is that it proposes a dynamic in which power shifts; this point is particularly relevant to the teacher of adults as many andragogical principles and strategies aim to foster learner empowerment and promote the development of the self-directed adult learner (Booth, 2007). Daloz (1999) contends that as a student and a teacher get to know each other better over time, the distance between the two narrows. "As greater intimacy develops, some of the students' unreflecting deference to authority may diminish. No longer based on superficial trappings [and, we add, inauthentic boundaries], the relationship has the potential to be transformed into something more profound" (Daloz, 1999, p. 124) in support of learning and change. In the deliberate relationship framework, our work "purposefully supports students' increasing ability to claim power over time" based on the students' changes in "expertise, independence, and comprehension of the complexity of knowledge" (Tom, 1997, p. 16). This is the key, however: this shift needs to be based on students' developmental readiness and not professors' agendas, a perspective consistent with theories about adult development and learning (Kegan, 1994, 2000; Taylor, Marienau, and Fiddler, 2000; Drago-Severson; 2004; Taylor, 2006) and transformative learning (Daloz, 1986; Mezirow, 1991, 2000; Cranton, 1994; Daloz, 1999).

The deliberate relationship framework offers opportunities to carefully consider when we might want to work close to an established boundary or even shift it by facilitating a "genuine and controlled" (Tom, 1997, p. 12) relationship with our learners. Some boundary revisions may be quite helpful and appropriate as long as they do not take advantage of students' trust in us (Barnett, 2008). Additionally, Tom (1997) proposes that we can model the decision making that occurs in the pause between impulse and action by making our intentions and practices transparent to our students by explaining to them what we are doing and why. By developing our own intentional practice and being transparent when we do work close to or alter existing or traditional boundaries, we continue to develop our own capacity to think through new and different boundary-related conundrums that emerge.

Strategies for Boundary Setting in Relational Teaching and Deliberate Relationships

A relational approach and the deliberate relationship framework reveal the importance of reconsidering the boundaries between us and our adult

MELANIE BOOTH, EdD, is the dean of learning and assessment and director of the Center for Experiential Learning and Assessment at Marylhurst University in Oregon.

HARRIET L. SCHWARTZ, PhD, is an assistant professor in the School of Education at Carlow University in Pittsburgh.

NEW DIRECTIONS FOR TEACHING AND LEARNING • DOI: 10.1002/tl

5

This chapter explores international students' perspectives of boundaries in the American graduate-level classroom, specifically considering the culturally based essence of boundaries.

The Coconut and the Peach: Understanding, Establishing, and Maintaining Interpersonal Boundaries with International Students

Miki Yamashita, Harriet L. Schwartz

International students come to the United States not only to attain their educational degrees but also to develop their careers. Faculty members can provide social and emotional support that will help students overcome culture shock and adjust to graduate student life, thus increasing students' potential to succeed academically and to develop as emerging professionals. International students, especially at the graduate level, are adult learners. They bring their prior experience of teacher–student relationships from academic cultures of their home countries, which sometimes can cause cultural misunderstandings between them and their professors in higher education institutions in the United States. To understand our adult learners, generally speaking, faculty members need to connect with them, respect them, acknowledge their experience, and value these learners as knowers (Brookfield, 1993). To achieve this level of understanding with international graduate students, American teachers must intentionally strive to learn more about these students' backgrounds and learning styles.

However, the literature indicates a lack of attention to international students in U.S. classrooms, suggesting that international students lack quality support in their study abroad experiences (Thompson and Thompson, 1996; Trice, 2001; Andrade, 2006). Research has shown that faculty

NEW DIRECTIONS FOR TEACHING AND LEARNING, no. 131, Fall 2012 © Wiley Periodicals, Inc.
Published online in Wiley Online Library (wileyonlinelibrary.com) • DOI: 10.1002/tl.20027

57

members are not always familiar with ways to resolve problems that international students present (Cooper, 1983; Kaplan, 1987; Selvadurai, 1992; Light, 1993; Trice, 2001). In one study (Thompson and Thompson, 1996), faculty members overwhelmingly reported that international students did not ask for clarification of issues or assignments that were unclear. In addition, the faculty in the study reported that international students rarely debated issues in class, disagreed with the opinion of a classmate or instructor, or challenged the status quo. However, international students' reluctance to engage in the classroom may not indicate a lack of interest or commitment but rather may be an indication of cultural communication boundaries.

In this chapter, we explore the topic of interpersonal boundaries as it relates to international students. Given that we cannot consider this topic in the context of all international cultures, we instead focus on graduate-level Japanese international students. This population is particularly helpful in our consideration of boundaries because research suggests that Asian international students face a significant level of cultural adjustment when they study in the United States. All international students face challenges in U.S. higher education institutions, but the literature suggests that Asian international students have relatively more cultural adjustment challenges when studying in the United States than do, for example, many European international students (Zhang and Dixon, 2001) or those from other non-European cultures (for example, African) that may share similar educational systems. Faculty members indicate that international students from Asian countries in particular have problems related to language difficulties, while students from European countries often arrive with a better command of English and some shared cultural patterns that allow them to develop relationships with domestic students more easily (Trice, 2001). As an Asian country, Japan is culturally very different from the United States. These differences provide challenges as well as opportunities for students to grow. Our intention is that by exploring these questions in relation to Japanese students, we will help faculty develop awareness and strategies that can be used when considering international students from any culture.

In this chapter, we utilize intercultural communication concepts to explore how Japanese students may think about boundaries and interpersonal relationships with their American professors. In addition, we consider how differing perceptions among Japanese students and American professors may impede the development of quality collaborative relationships. Then we discuss how we as faculty might navigate these cultural differences with greater sensitivity and intentionality as we strive to improve our teaching practices. This chapter draws on Yamashita's dissertation, "Japanese International Graduate Students in U.S. Higher Education Classrooms: An Investigation of Their Pedagogical and Epistemological Challenges and Supports" (Yamashita, 2009).

NEW DIRECTIONS FOR TEACHING AND LEARNING • DOI: 10.1002/tl

Boundaries as Cultural Construct

Japanese students come from a group-oriented culture. So, we must rephrase "how to maintain interpersonal boundaries with students" to "how to build relationships with students." Generally speaking, Japanese students work from a relational frame of reference that values *dependence*, while American students work from a frame that values *independence*. Anthropologist Edward T. Hall (1976) introduced the concept of "low-context" versus "high-context" communication styles to capture differences in human relations. Nisbett (2003) contends that Western culture, such as U.S. American, is *low-context culture*, in which people tend to be independent from circumstances or particular personal relationships so that they are impermeable and can claim an independent self. Hall indicates that westerners tend to emphasize independence or detachment from one another to respect personal boundaries.

In contrast, according to Hall (1976), Eastern cultures, such as Japan's culture, belong to *high-context culture*, in which people tend to feel embedded in, and related to, a team or group. They decide how to communicate or relate to others depending on their hierarchical system in status, age, or social roles. Once a Japanese student becomes an in-group member with a teacher, the student takes advantage and uses *amae*. The word *amai* means "sweet." The literary translation of *amae* is "sweet dependency." It is a tendency to depend on somebody who is close to and older than oneself, such as a parent or teacher. In their teacher–student relationships, Japanese students' feelings of attachment and dependence on their teachers is often evident. Some Japanese students consult with their teacher even about private issues, such as breaking up with a partner. Therefore, Japanese teacher–student relationships focus on how to develop and maintain dependency rather than how to maintain boundaries as separate individuals.

Interestingly, the metaphors that are often used to contrast Japanese and American personalities are a coconut and a peach; these metaphors have also been used to describe differing relational styles between American culture and German culture (Zaninelli, 1994 [revised 2005]; Robinson, 2004). The coconut has a tough and not very appealing shell, but once you break through the exterior, it is soft inside—people share even their personal issues with you. Once you are accepted into the inner circle of the group, you are protected and supported. The peach, however, is soft, inviting, and easy to get into, but it has a hard core that is difficult to penetrate. The core represents privacy, which is to be respected as a personal boundary.

Referring to Hall's (1976) concept of low-context and high-context cultures, one of the American core values, "independence," separates each individual to maintain healthy relationships, and one of the Japanese core values, "relational," binds them to build interdependent relationships (even

NEW DIRECTIONS FOR TEACHING AND LEARNING • DOI: 10.1002/tl

in relationships wherein there is a power differential); this is a clear distinction between Japanese and American cultures.

Intercultural Misunderstandings Impede Faculty–Student Relationships

Collaborative work in the teacher–student relationship is a significant andragogical principle; however, when the students are international, both teachers and students may misunderstand each other, which can impede collaboration. When different cultures meet, misunderstandings may ensue. As Barna (1991) suggests, there are a variety of sources of misunderstandings, such as "assuming similarity instead of difference, language problems, nonverbal misunderstanding, the presence of preconceptions and stereotypes, the tendency to evaluate, and the high anxiety that often exists in intercultural encounters" (p. 343). Barna's statement suggests that teachers should look at the hidden part of cultures, such as cultural values and beliefs, when working with people from different cultures and backgrounds; doing this can mitigate cultural misunderstandings. However, cultural misunderstandings can occur easily as long as we remain unaware of our cultural lenses, or habit of mind, and cultural misunderstandings may impede quality teacher–student relationships with Japanese students.

Power and Distance. According to the metaphor of peach culture and coconut culture, Japanese students who came from a coconut culture tend to keep distance from their professors until they break the hard shell of the coconut. They cannot relax and talk to their professors like their American peers do, until they feel that they are invited, by their professor, into the professor's personal boundary space. Japanese students perceive that American students appear to talk to their professors in an equal and frank manner. Japanese students also identify egalitarianism in American teacher–student relationships, which for many Japanese students is a new experience that requires adaptation. Due to this cultural difference, misunderstandings in teacher–student relationships may occur.

In Yamashita's dissertation research (2009), Mari, a thirty-five-year-old Japanese female student in a first-year doctoral program in education, said that building good relationships with her professor was not easy. Due to her prior experience at a university in the Japanese high power-distance culture, she felt awkward when considering calling her professors by their first names, as her American classmates did. *Power distance* is defined as "the extent to which the less powerful members of institutions and organizations within a country expect and accept that power is distributed unequally" (Hofstede, 1991, p. 28). In U.S. higher education institutions, students are encouraged not only to develop academic competence but also "to demonstrate interactional competence in social settings in order to do well in school" (Gilmore, 1985, p. 139). However, the large power-distance cultural tendency in this case made Mari hesitate to interact with her professors. Her teachers may have interpreted this kind of attitude as disinterest in the class or the teacher–student relationship.

Hofstede explains that most group-oriented cultures, such as Japanese, maintain large power distances, and a teacher–student relationship still tends to be power over rather than power with. According to Chen (1999), Biggs (1996), and Yuen and Lee (1994), in larger power-distance cultures such as in Japan, the teacher controls the power in the classroom. Students hesitate to assert their opinions or express their doubts and disagree with the teacher because they view teachers as symbols of authority. In this large power-distance culture, once students break through the hard coconut shell, they can create an *amae* relationship with their professor that allows them to be more forthcoming and disclose themselves in the relationship. This Japanese process of forming a teacher–student relationship may not be understood easily by American professors.

Lack of Empathy. In Yamashita's dissertation research (2009), Asami, a twenty-seven-year-old, third-year student pursuing a master's in conflict resolution, shared her experience. Asami was more outspoken than most other students in the study. She said that her professor did not show empathy when she expressed concern about her experience in the classroom. She tried to participate in class discussions to get credit, and in one case she kept her hand raised for more than twenty minutes, but some students dominated the class conversation and her professor never called on her. She visited the professor's office and told him that she raised her hand for a long time and asked why he did not give her a chance to talk. The professor said to her that he did not see her hand and that she should have said "Excuse me" to get his attention. Asami told the professor that it was a big effort for her as an international student to raise a hand. Then the professor said to her that she was naive to expect help from others in a graduate-level class in the United States, and if he were in Japan, he would follow Japanese ways, so Asami should follow American ways: "When in Rome, do as the Romans do." Asami left the meeting discouraged from trying to continue engaging in class discussion.

Asami's professor did not recognize her effort but merely asserted that she should try harder and should simply conform to U.S. cultural expectations regarding the classroom. He failed to understand that even if Asami wanted to conform (and in the case of this example, she was trying to be more assertive), her contextual understanding of his response would still be shaped by her cultural framework. That is, adapting to U.S. culture is not as simple as being willing to change; it also may require major shifts in how one even understands a situation. M. J. Bennett (1972) asserts that sympathy is inadequate in intercultural communication, but not empathy. *Sympathy* is "the imaginative placing of ourselves in another person's position" (p. 66). That is, "we are not taking the role of another person or imaging how the other person thinks and feels, but rather we are referencing how we ourselves might think or feel in similar circumstances."

NEW DIRECTIONS FOR TEACHING AND LEARNING • DOI: 10.1002/tl

Empathy is, however, "how we might imagine the thoughts and feelings of other people from their own perspectives" (M. J. Bennett, 1998, p. 197). The idea of empathy is similar to the *Platinum Rule*: "Do unto others as they would do unto themselves" and the idea of sympathy is related to the Golden Rule, "Do unto others as you would have them do unto you," as M. J. Bennett suggested. Asami was trying to cross the cultural gap and yet she experienced no empathy from her professor.

The example of Asami and her professor may seem extreme to some faculty members who genuinely try to help international students adjust to the U.S. classroom. For these professors, the example may serve as a reminder that many of our international students may have encountered professors like Asami's prior to entering our classroom; these students may have been previously dismissed by professors who were unwilling to cross the cultural gap, and, thus, they may be hesitant to engage. Even as we bring our best efforts to our classrooms, we must remember that our students carry with them their prior experiences with a range of professors. A student's hesitancy to engage might have very little to do with the environment that we are trying to create and much more to do with her or his prior experience; knowing this will help us be more empathic as we work to bridge the cultural gap.

Casual Conversation and Perceived Superficial Relationships.
Americans commonly engage in casual conversational back-and-forth that includes statements that are not always intended literally. For example, Americans might ask "How are you doing?" and not really expect an honest or complete answer. Similarly, Americans might say "We should meet for coffee sometime" but not really intend to set up the meeting. This American *ritual talk* is intended to acknowledge the other and is sometimes misunderstood by Japanese students who perceive it as superficial. The idea of communication rituals discussed by Tannen (1994) and Goffman (1971) refers to social interactions that take on the quality of a ritual, repeated and well defined, in a cultural group. These may include, for example, greeting rituals, argument rituals, and compliment rituals. In Yamashita's first year of studying in a graduate program in the United States, she was puzzled by professors' friendliness and their *ritual talk*. In her graduate program, she often encountered two of her female professors on campus. They repeatedly said to her that "We should go out for tea" and yet, during her six years of study, this never happened. People in the United States might say "We should go out for coffee or tea sometime!" and while this means that they are interested in getting together with you, it does not express any obligation for follow-up. From a Japanese perspective, however, this kind of statement tends to be taken as guaranteed and becomes an obligation.

Japanese students who are looking for help, friendship, or social support might be disappointed when that suggested meeting does not happen, and they may infer that Americans are superficial. American people from low-context culture sometimes use ritual talk, such as "What's going on with you?" to warm up a conversation; in such cases, the phrase does not really mean anything more than a greeting. American culture is a mobility culture, and people enjoy communicating even with strangers, but this small talk may be understood as superficial by people from high-context cultures. Professors need to be careful not to use this ritual talk with international students; otherwise, students may doubt their sincerity. A student who perceives a professor to be insincere may be less likely to seek help from that professor. In addition, when a professor makes ritual talk, such as "We should meet for coffee sometime" with a Japanese student, the student may believe that she or he has established connection with that faculty member or may anticipate a supportive relationship and thus may not seek other sources of support. However, if the professor does not follow up and actually invite the student to meet, the student may move through the semester feeling isolated.

Experiences of Exclusion and Belonging. Feelings of belonging are a necessity for international students. These feelings also help them to have a quality teacher–student relationship. Japanese students sometimes cannot join class discussion due to their lack of knowledge of American cultural references, such as historical events, pop culture, and slang, which make them feel like outsiders. Jiro, a twenty-seven-year-old male and third-year doctoral student in public affairs and a participant in Yamashita's dissertation research (2009), had been living and working in the United States for more than six years and was fluent in English, but he still could not join the class discussions. Because of that, he felt that he was not welcomed by the group, and he shut himself out from his peers as well as his professors. Jiro said that, in class, people mainly discussed domestic rather than international issues. What he could do was to share his Japanese perspective, but he hesitated to do that because he was not sure if his professor and American peers would appreciate it.

Moreover, he could not adapt to the quick turn-taking in class discussion. In high-context cultures such as Japanese culture, context is important (Nisbett, 2003). Context is formed by people, so students tend to stick with one topic rather than changing topics frequently. Therefore, Japanese students do not value bringing up unrelated topics in a classroom discussion. In contrast, in low-context cultures, such as U.S. culture, people tend to be independent from the context so that they can claim their voice. Jiro said that his American peers did not hesitate to voice their opinions even when they were not related to the class discussion. Because people wanted to talk about themselves, they kept talking with almost no pause, and the discussion topics kept changing. As a consequence, he kept missing his chance to jump in and participate. This made him feel like an outsider.

Missing the opportunity to speak up in class deepened Jiro's feelings of not belonging to the class. He said that every time he missed a chance to contribute to class discussions, he felt that he received small jabs to his stomach, and he experienced increased stress. Jiro said that he wanted his

NEW DIRECTIONS FOR TEACHING AND LEARNING • DOI: 10.1002/tl

professors to ask him questions that related to Japan. Cress (1999) asserts that in the collegiate environment, it is crucial for each student to feel important and cared for by others, and students must have a sense of belonging to grow, develop, and succeed. The sense of belonging can give international students feelings of security, which can be a solid foundation for a quality teacher–student relationship and contribute well to student learning.

Navigating Interpersonal Boundaries Across Cultures: Strategies for Faculty

As previously discussed, boundaries are culturally constructed, so various intercultural misunderstandings may occur and may negatively influence the teacher–student relationship. Based on these discussions, we would like to propose five strategies to help professors and students create mutually understood expectations regarding interpersonal boundaries:

1. Increase intercultural competence
2. Provide a sense of inclusion
3. Create transparency of mutual expectations
4. Offer acknowledgment and understanding
5. Balance: Honor the self and the other

Strategy 1: Empathy as Intercultural Competence. It is not an overstatement to say that empathy is one of the most important skills for a professor who seeks to develop positive academic relationships with international students. "In empathy, one attends to the feelings of another; in sympathy, one attends the suffering of another, but the feelings are one's own" (Wispé, 1968, p. 441). Empathizing with another by attending to her feelings is not easy to do, particularly with those who are from different cultures, but J. M. Bennett (1998) suggests these practices: be curious, think flexibly, be motivated, and be open-minded. She calls these approaches *the heart set: affective competence* (p. 20). She argues that these abilities of intercultural competence allow us to communicate effectively and appropriately in a variety of cultural contexts. In addition, Pusch (1981) defines a collection of related personality characteristics that contribute to intercultural competence.

An effective cross-cultural communicator is often described as a person who has rather vague boundaries of self; who tolerates ambiguity well; and who is adaptable to new stimuli, social conventions, and behavioral demands. The person is skillful at observing and interpreting the cultural features of behavior and displaying respect for other cultures and their people. Finally, this person is able to accept his or her failures, and understand his or her cultural roots and their effect on personal behavior (Pusch, 1981).

NEW DIRECTIONS FOR TEACHING AND LEARNING • DOI: 10.1002/tl

Developing empathy as a cultural competence requires strong yet flexible boundaries, openness, and sensitivity.

Strategy 2: Providing Sense of Inclusion for Japanese Students. Japanese students from a high-context culture tend to appreciate a sense of inclusion and the feeling of belonging to a group. Simply greeting Japanese students with nonverbal gestures or checking on how they are doing before or after class is very important. In Yamashita's dissertation (2009), Taro, a twenty-seven-year-old male who majored in Japanese, shared his feeling of being supported by his professor. He said, "My professor says *Ohayo* (good morning) or *Konnichiwa* (hello) to me in Japanese. I like that." By initiating conversation with international students, professors can build and maintain relationships, which may help these students to manage social interactions and anxiety.

Making eye contact with students in lectures and listening to them attentively by nodding and smiling also expresses care and gives them a sense of inclusion. Doing this not only helps students feel comfortable approaching their professors but also creates a welcoming environment that helps bridge the power distance culture gap. Additionally, Japanese students appreciate when a professor defines jargon or slang used in class. When professors help students understand cultural references and inside jokes, international students are more likely to experience a sense of belonging. They feel part of the group when they can laugh with their classmates. To promote cultural exchange, the professor can also ask Japanese students if they have similar jargon or slang in their cultures, further enhancing a sense of inclusion.

With this foundation, we can learn about each Japanese student and her or his background. Even students from Japanese cultures have individual approaches, timing, and comfort zones about their boundaries. By initiating and making small talk with each individual Japanese student, professors and their Japanese students have a chance to create balanced teacher–student relationships.

Strategy 3: Transparency of Mutual Expectations. Due to cultural differences and expectation differences, Japanese students may unintentionally violate their professor's personal boundary. To attempt to prevent this, it is crucial for professors to be clear about their personal boundaries and expectations of students. For example, professors should be clear about office hours and other availability and contact information.

A Japanese student who is attempting to bridge the power divide as she or he perceives her American classmates doing may contact a professor at a time that the professor considers to be inappropriate. In this case, a compassionate clarification regarding appropriate contact will enhance the relationship. Conversely, if the professor assumes the student is simply inconsiderate and responds from that perspective, the professor may shame a student who will then avoid further contact with professors, even when she or he needs help. Similarly, a Japanese student who feels connected with a faculty mentor may disclose personal information beyond what the professor is accustomed to hearing from American students. Again, compassionate clarification and transparency of role expectations can preserve and even enhance the relationship as well as the student's cultural competency.

To know students' side expectations, conducting "a minute paper" at the end of class was appreciated by international students in Yamashita's (2009) study. In a minute paper, students take a few minutes to write comments and any questions for the professor. This paper can be used as feedback for the professor or a communication tool between a professor and students to get to know students' expectations of their professors.

Assigning longer reflection papers, which are reports of self-reflection based on a topic the professor chooses, are also helpful for both Japanese students and professors to enhance mutual understanding. Japanese students can share their feelings and thoughts in a constructive way with their professors, and the professors can learn about what their students are going through, which may help the professors to be accepting and compassionate.

Strategy 4: Acknowledgment and Understanding. It is sometimes stressful for individuals when their ethnic identity is not acknowledged. In Yamashita's dissertation (2009), Jiro said he was stressed and sad that his identity was not acknowledged as Japanese but just as an Asian American by his professor and peers. Barna (as cited in J. M. Bennett, 1998) suggests that "[if you] become secure in your own identity … there is little chance for serious loss of self-esteem and more freedom for open investigation" (p. 220). Japanese students who experience a sense of respect from their professors may be more open to learning.

Jiro's professors could ask him about Japanese culture and its values to acknowledge his Japanese identity. International students appreciate when a professor becomes curious about international issues. Students then can share their perspectives and experience in class and be satisfied by contributing to the class discussion. This cultural exchange promotes mutual acknowledgment among teachers and students.

Strategy 5: Balancing Act—Honoring the Self and the Other. One of the challenges in seeking to be more culturally aware and inclusive regarding international students is that sometimes an approach that honors the student's home culture conflicts with our own cultural norms regarding appropriate boundaries. These situations call for deep reflection: Is the student's cultural norm simply different from my own and thus uncomfortable but ultimately appropriate? Or is the student's norm in conflict with my core values and sense of what is appropriate? An example of the former is that I, as a professor, may not be accustomed to asking international students to share their culture in class, yet I may determine that this is an appropriate strategy. Conversely, a Japanese student whom I mentor may disclose a personal struggle that I feel ill equipped to deal with. In the first case, it is appropriate for me to attempt to stretch my comfort zone and explore a new approach. In the second example, I must honor my own personal boundary and sense of my capabilities. In this case, I can respond to the student with compassionate clarity and transparency regarding my role and help her or him seek appropriate support. Balancing our own cultural norms with others' is not a simple matter. However, deep reflection can help us decide when to stretch and when to hold our boundaries.

Concluding Thoughts

It is not always easy to be mindful and sensitive when we communicate with people from different cultures. "When we communicate mindlessly, we do not notice the distinctive qualities of the cultural person with whom we are communicating. Rather, we fall back on our stereotypes to reduce our guesswork" (Ting-Toomey and Chung, 2005, p. 44). It requires extra effort for faculty members to build and maintain teacher–student relationships with international students, but it will be an opportunity for faculty to develop their intercultural competence. As Ting-Toomey (1999) states, "[f]rom a human creativity standpoint, we learn more from people who are different from us than from those who are similar to us" (p. 8).

International students under stress appreciate meaningful relationships with faculty, such as when faculty members mentor students regarding their professional development. If faculty members can enhance their intercultural competencies and deepen their cognitive, affective, and behavioral understanding of Japanese students, it is possible to minimize intercultural misunderstanding, enhance mutual understanding, and create quality teacher–student relationships.

References

Andrade, M. S. "International Student Persistence: Integration or Cultural Integrity." *Journal of College Student Retention, Research, Theory & Practice*, 2006, 8(1) 57–81.

Barna, L. M. "Stumbling Blocks in Intercultural Communication." In L. A. Samovar and R. E. Porter (eds.), *Intercultural Communication: A Reader.* Belmont, Calif.: Wadsworth, 1991.

Bennett, J. M. "Transition Shock: Putting Culture Shock in Perspective." In M. J. Bennett (ed.), *Basic Concept of Intercultural Communication: Selected Readings.* Yarmouth, Maine: Intercultural Press, 1998.

Bennett, M. J. "Empathic Perception: The Operation of Self-Awareness in Human Perception." Unpublished master's thesis, San Francisco State University, 1972.

Bennett, M. J. "Intercultural Communication: A Current Perspective." In M. J. Bennett (ed.), *Basic Concept of Intercultural Communication: Selected Readings.* Yarmouth, Maine: Intercultural Press, 1998.

Biggs, J. "Western Misperceptions of the Confucian-Heritage Learning Culture." In D. A. Watkins and J. B. Biggs (eds.), *The Chinese Learner: Cultural, Psychological and Contextual Influences.* Hong Kong: Central Printing Press, 1996.

Brookfield, S. "Self-Directed Learning, Political Clarity, and the Critical Practice of Adult Education." *Adult Education Quarterly*, 1993, *43*(4), 227–242.

Chen, C. P. "Common Stressors Among International College Students: Research and Counseling Implications." *Journal of College Counseling*, 1999, 2, 49–65.

Cooper, K. J. "Increasing the International Relevance of U.S. Education." In H. M. Jenkins and Associates (eds.), *Educating Students from Other Nations: American Colleges and Universities in International Educational Interchange*. San Francisco: Jossey-Bass, 1983.

Cress, C. "The Impact of Campus Climate on Students' Cognitive and Affective Development." Unpublished doctoral dissertation, University of California at Los Angeles, 1999.

Gilmore, P. "Silence and Sulking: Emotional Displays in the Classroom." In M. Saville-Troike and H. Giles (eds.), *Intergroup Behavior*. Oxford: Basil Blackwell, 1985.

Goffman, E. *Relations in Public: Microstudies of the Public Order*. New York: Harper & Row, 1971.

Hall, E. T. *Beyond Culture*. New York: Anchor Books, 1976.

Hofstede, G. *Cultures and Organizations: Software of the Mind*. London: McGraw-Hill, 1991.

Kaplan, R. B. "Foreign Students: Developing Institutional Policy." *College Board Review*, 1987, *143*, 7–9, 28–30.

Light, T. "Erasing Borders: The Changing Role of American Higher Education in the World." *European Journal of Education*, 1993, *28*, 253–271.

Nisbett, R. E. *The Geography of Thought: How Asians and Westerners Think Different and Why*. London: Nicholas Brealey, 2003.

Pusch, M. D. *Multicultural Education*. New York: Intercultural Network, 1981.

Robinson, H. "Peach and Coconut Communicate: A Training Exercise." *SIETAR Europa & Global Hub Newsletter*, March 2004. Retrieved from http://www.sietar-europa.org /about_us/Newsletter/Mar04/Peach&CoconutCommunicate.html.

Selvadurai, R. "Problems Faced by International Students in American Colleges and Universities." *Community Review*, 1992, *12*(1–2), 27–32.

Tannen, D. *Talking from 9 to 5: How Women's and Men's Conversational Styles Affect Who Gets Heard, Who Gets the Credit, and What Gets Done at Work*. New York: William Morrow, 1994.

Thompson, H. B., and Thompson, G. H. "Confronting Diversity Issues in the Classroom with Strategies to Improve Satisfaction and Retention of International Students." *Journal of Education for Business*, 1996, *72*(1), 53–55.

Ting-Toomey, S. *Communication Across Cultures*. New York: Guilford Press, 1999.

Ting-Toomey, S., and Chung, L. C. *Understanding Intercultural Communication*. Los Angeles: Roxbury, 2005.

Trice, A. G. "Faculty Perceptions of Graduate International Students: The Benefits and Challenges." Paper presented at the twenty-sixth annual meeting of the Association for the Study of Higher Education, Richmond, Va., November 15–18, 2001.

Wispé, L. G. "Sympathy and Empathy." In D. L. Sills (ed.), *International Encyclopedia of the Social Sciences*. New York: Macmillan, 1968.

Yamashita, M. "Japanese International Graduate Students in U.S. Higher Education Classrooms: An Investigation of Their Pedagogical and Epistemological Challenges and Supports." Unpublished doctoral dissertation, Portland State University, Portland, Ore., 2009.

Yuen, C., and Lee, S. N. "Applicability of the Learning Style Inventory in an Asian Context and Its Predictive Value." *Educational and Psychological Measurement*, 1994, *54*(2), 541–549.

Zaninelli, S. M. "What Happens when 'Coconut' and 'Peach' Communicate, or: The World's Greatest Misunderstanding on Interpersonal Distance USA–Germany."

Retrieved from http://www.culture-contact.com/fileadmin/files/coconut_und_peach_engl.pdf

Zhang, N., and Dixon, D. N. "Multiculturally Responsive Counseling: Effects on Asian Students' Ratings of Counselors." *Journal of Multicultural Counseling & Development*, 2001, 29(4), 253–262.

MIKI YAMASHITA, EdD, is an associate professor, Department of Economics and Business Administration at Reitaku University in Chiba, Japan.

HARRIET L. SCHWARTZ, PhD, is an assistant professor in the School of Education at Carlow University in Pittsburgh.

NEW DIRECTIONS FOR TEACHING AND LEARNING • DOI: 10.1002/tl

6

Providing guidance for graduate teaching assistants on how to establish boundaries is critical to support their teaching and research responsibilities and to advance their professional development.

Complicity or Multiplicity? Defining Boundaries for Graduate Teaching Assistant Success

Karen Dunn-Haley, Anne Zanzucchi

Professional development of graduate teaching assistants (GTAs) regarding interpersonal boundaries is key not only to the well-being of the GTAs but also to the undergraduates they are teaching. GTAs who are developing their professional identities are a primary contact for undergraduates, especially in lower-division classes, and thus play a key role in undergraduate student academic success and retention.

At public four-year institutions, graduate students make up 15 percent of the instructional staff (National Center for Education Statistics, 2010). At research universities, this number triples as graduate students can be responsible for a significant fraction of the undergraduate instruction (Austin, 2002). It is difficult to quantify the instructional role of GTAs; however, as one example, at the University of Michigan (AY 2006–2007), graduate students taught 41 percent of lower-division courses either individually or with a faculty member. GTAs have particularly high impact in introductory science courses, staffing more than two-thirds of laboratory sections (National Center for Education Statistics, 2010). Because instructor contact is among the predictors of undergraduate success (Pascarella and Terenzi, 1991; Tinto, 1997), clearly, GTAs, as the first point of contact, play a critical role in undergraduate persistence and retention. Further, an initial study in science, technology, math, and engineering fields show that graduate student instructors, through informal mentoring and role modeling, may even

New Directions for Teaching and Learning, no. 131, Fall 2012 © Wiley Periodicals, Inc.
Published online in Wiley Online Library (wileyonlinelibrary.com) • DOI: 10.1002/tl.20028

influence undergraduate students' major degree aspirations (O'Neal and others, 2007). As GTAs are a statistically significant instructional workforce with high levels of contact with undergraduates, their professional development training is a high institutional priority.

Direction in establishing boundaries with undergraduates, peers, and faculty advisers is a key component of overall GTA training. Graduate students, as researchers, instructors, and students themselves, have a diverse set of responsibilities that are often simultaneously at play. Establishing boundaries between these diverse roles is an important step toward claiming a professional identity. How GTAs stake out boundaries, with, for example, a classroom presence, affects not only instructional effectiveness but also their well-being and progress to degree. Several studies have indicated that confidence and authority in the classroom is just as important to effective teaching as pedagogical skills and content knowledge (Prieto and Altmaier, 1994). Lovitts's research (2001) on graduate retention points to difficult classroom experiences as a contributing factor leading to degree program departure. Other research suggests that pedagogical training has highest impact among less experienced teachers in terms of instilling confidence, creativity, and efficacy, which underscores the importance of instructional development support at the beginning of a career (Gibbs and Coffey, 2000). As this chapter illustrates, this early professional development also should address boundary issues to help GTAs build and assert their professional identities inside and outside of the classroom.

Many novice teachers begin their careers by replicating teaching practices they experienced as students, or "cultural scripting" that is mediated over time by formal training (Stigler and Hiebert, 1999; Helterbran, 2008). GTAs need to recognize previous training or experiences to intentionally construct their own teaching personae based on their discipline, personality, and newly acquired pedagogical skills. Helterbran's examination of the positive and negative teacher qualities, reflected on Ratemyprofessors.com, reveals the importance of instructor self-awareness. Professional developers have a role helping GTAs recognize that "personal characteristics . . . are integral in the overall portrait of a professional teacher" (Helterbran, 2008, p. 126). New GTAs should understand the potential impact on instruction of personal choices—for instance, the decisions they make regarding attire and levels of self-disclosure. Roach (1997) has connected less classroom misbehavior to more formal instructor attire. Gorham, Cohen, and Morris's later study (1999) complicates Roach's conclusion by examining whether casual attire leads students to rate instructors as more extroverted (and presumably more approachable). Allitt (2005) details how formality, professional distance, and structure in his classroom led to effective learning and engagement. In contrast, Mazer, Murphy, and Simonds's preliminary experiments (2009) with disclosure levels on Facebook suggest that high levels of disclosure lead to greater instructor credibility.

The variation in this research and its preliminary nature suggests that professional development should present choices and guide new GTAs as they develop a teaching style and form of self-presentation with which they are comfortable. In general, scholars writing about teaching effectiveness connect clear boundaries and the development of a teaching persona to effective instruction (Parini, 2004; Lang, 2008). Considering the implicit connection among confidence, authority, and clear boundaries, GTAs who intentionally construct a "teaching persona" and maintain classroom boundaries are more likely to become effective instructors.

Introduction, Institutional Context

Supporting GTAs' progress toward developing a professional identity often involves many mentors, including seminar leaders, graduate student peers, dissertation advisers, instructors of record, and teaching and learning experts. As a new research campus (2005), the University California (UC) at Merced is relatively small (approximately 5,000 total students), which has allowed the Center for Research on Teaching Excellence (CRTE) staff to work closely with a majority of the graduate student and faculty population. UC Merced's newness and size, combined with an increasing population of graduate students, offers a unique opportunity to examine graduate student training challenges and to view nationwide trends in a microcosm.

How the CRTE has responded to GTA professional development is multifaceted, as we work with incoming graduate students at orientation, in workshops throughout their academic careers, and during the advanced-to-candidacy stage with an instructional intern and Fund for the Improvement of Postsecondary Education (FIPSE) grant program. In all facets of graduate training, boundary issues have emerged as a central element. Referencing qualitative data from surveys and pre- and post-workshop reflections, this chapter summarizes the GTA programs and professional development workshop materials and explains the connection to an understanding of boundaries—between GTAs and students as well as faculty and peers. These workshop materials translate broadly into instructional support activities such as orientations, pedagogy courses, consultations, and mentoring. Our overall focus, through specific examples and curriculum, will be on ways that faculty and staff mentors can guide graduate students toward forming a scholarly, reflexive identity as future faculty.

General Problem

A very young GTA begins class with a summary of the lecture just given by a senior professor. Throwing out some slang and colorful language, the GTA makes it clear that she can level with the undergraduates and is more "hip" than the professor.

Acting complicit with her students could make the GTA seem approachable, and, by attracting more students to office hours, the GTA might facilitate learning. However, the GTA faces a multiplicity of roles; she is someone who in the future might be asked for a recommendation by a student; she will be giving grades and setting standards. She is a future colleague of the senior professor. New scholars inside and outside of academia struggle to construct a professional demeanor; how can they be friendly with colleagues and those they teach and at the same time serve multiple professional responsibilities? Most graduate students are students and instructors at the same time, and they also are competing with and seeking support from peers. Adding significant stress, unlike a worker in an office cubicle, they are on a classroom stage. Hence, training that assists GTAs to grapple with professional boundaries with their students, faculty, and peers is critical to their success with instruction and future employment.

Some boundaries have fairly obvious legal parameters, which are relatively simple to explore through interactive online or in-person workshops. For example, according to national studies on sexual harassment policy, more than 80 percent of public four-year institutions have a well-documented policy and grievance procedure with related outreach (Robertson, Dyer, and Campbell, 1988). Offering interactive presentations can engage GTAs in understanding important policies and procedures. In our boundaries training, we have encouraged GTAs to read key passages aloud to underscore the importance of policy that might likely be skimmed in the best of circumstances. In addition to workshops, many institutions are using independently provided online training to document training in sexual harassment policy. A more complex and ongoing type of training involves assisting GTAs to shape professional personae that suit their personalities and facilitate student learning. Boundary issues can emerge as GTAs contemplate how to communicate online, how to use humor, and how to be approachable yet maintain authority.

Instilling Professional Identity at New GTA Orientation

A full or half-day of teaching orientation for new graduate students at a research university offers an opportunity to immediately acquaint these students, some of whom are transitioning from their undergraduate careers, with an understanding of their place in the profession as teachers and as researchers. Even graduate students with master's degrees or extensive professional experience are learning about discipline-specific scholarly conventions and a new campus culture. International students usually make up about one-third of an incoming graduate population; their transitions may resemble those of their American peers and are overlaid by an additional cultural transition (Rice and others, 2009). (For additional consideration of boundaries and international students, see Chapter Five of this sourcebook.)

As at many institutions, orientation begins with a lead campus administrator providing cautionary tales and insights into the balance between research and teaching during a graduate career. Establishing the boundaries between research and teaching is one component of GTAs' future success. This opening reflection from a senior administrator about balance is the beginning of a mentoring relationship, in that senior faculty are immediately demonstrating approachability and sharing extensive professional insight into degree completion. The orientation activities focus on classroom management, particularly how to handle the first day of class, which also underscores the need to establish clear boundaries and expectations with students.

Experienced GTAs, who have applied to be instructional interns within the CRTE, consult with professional staff to deliver the orientation. During the course of orientation, they model a range of presentation styles. In one segment on how to approach the first day of class, they have developed short video vignettes of a particularly bad start to a class and a contrasting better beginning. Although we typically would not endorse a good–bad logic to teaching, the videos are a source of humor that relieve tension about establishing a rapport with undergraduates. These experienced GTAs lead a discussion of the main components of a first class session by conducting a think-pair-share activity about three outcomes: building community in the classroom, setting classroom policies and academic expectations, and encouraging engagement outside the classroom (clubs, office hours, for example). After goals are established, the first video is shown of a GTA fumbling through making class introductions, explaining the syllabus, and setting class policy, including covering institutional policies involving disability support services. Considering the goals of each process, new GTAs continue to work in pairs to identify what could be strengthened in the example. To conclude the training, the second vignette of a more successful first-day presentation is played, and the larger group discusses what makes it more successful. In the course of the discussion, experienced GTAs model how to handle a classroom in a professional manner.

The orientation provides opportunity for further dialogue with a panel of experienced GTAs, who discuss the particulars of establishing boundaries with undergraduates and developing a professional identity. Classroom attire is invariably discussed, for example, and some experienced GTAs have offered that they dress "a little bit better" on days they are teaching in part to establish authority. Other topics typically include time management, instructor of record conflicts, and grading practices. A dialogue regarding office hours also provides ample opportunity to discuss boundaries. Experienced GTAs encourage undergraduates to come in groups to office hours to conquer shyness and fear and to benefit from the questions posed by

NEW DIRECTIONS FOR TEACHING AND LEARNING • DOI: 10.1002/tl

peers. "Leave the office door open" or "Consider meeting at a public spot" are frequent suggestions, and a debate sometimes ensues about just how much of a "friend" a GTA can be to a student.

Most experienced GTAs underscore the importance of establishing approachability while maintaining some professional distance. Technology offers new opportunities to connect with undergraduates as well. GTAs typically advise keeping all e-mail correspondence friendly but formal, with clear guidelines about response time and style. Similarly, Facebook interaction benefits from some academic parameters, such as separate classroom spaces or the withholding of friend requests until the conclusion of the course. In contrast to recent research on the positive impact on credibility of self-disclosure on Facebook (Mazer, Murphy, and Simonds, 2009), experienced GTAs might warn against full self-disclosure or recount stories of the loss of credibility if they admit to not fully knowing the subject. (For additional consideration of boundaries and social media, see Chapter Two of this sourcebook.) Acknowledging that good teachers are always learning, experienced GTAs and professional staff point to practical solutions, such as promising to return to the student's question in the next class or giving the student responsibility for looking up the answer and bringing it back to class.

These panel discussions provide graduate students with important opportunities to consider the complexity of self-presentation in classroom and online. In the dialogue that takes place, experienced GTAs convey the message that choosing what to disclose and how to disclose it has an impact on teaching effectiveness. Overall, these orientation activities model multiple ways to be an effective teacher. International graduate students, for example, have the opportunity to engage with their experienced counterparts who can reflect on cultural transitions. As the think-pair-share activities move to the larger class discussion, something even more simple and powerful is revealed: new GTAs can see how a range of personalities engage with the same challenges through different, equally valid avenues.

Challenging Boundaries to Meet Advanced Graduate Students' Needs

In the process of completing dissertations, advanced graduate students struggle with several key aspects of academic work life that can challenge personal boundaries. After producing original research, often a solitary effort, they must learn to deal with the critiques of committee members and the publication peer review process. To better prepare future faculty, the CRTE has reached out to students in the dissertation stage, when they are likely to become isolated, to involve them in a larger learning community. As Lovitt's research (2001) on graduate retention suggests, this type of involvement can enhance retention and completion. The CRTE's efforts also have responded to feedback from a recent needs assessment that suggests faculty see a need for graduate students to learn to take criticism, "to develop a tougher skin." A lack of experience with handling written and oral criticism can affect the interpersonal relations between faculty mentors and advisees and affect time to degree. Collaboration with peers and faculty through the Guidebook Project—a program funded through a special topics FIPSE grant—has offered graduate students the opportunity to practice peer review, to handle criticism, and to develop professional boundaries. With research fellowship appointments and minigrants, we have initiated a grant-funded pilot project to support advanced graduate students in a learning community focused on publishable classroom and program assessment projects. The grant funds research positions for graduate students to participate in a scholarship of teaching and learning community, conduct action research by assessing classroom learning, and publish a resulting report and curriculum on e-scholarship (see http://escholarship.org/uc/crte_gsiguidebook).

One fundamental goal of this initiative is to provide highly experienced GTAs with classroom research opportunities, a process that begins to blur traditional distinctions between teaching and research. Similarly, dissolving disciplinary boundaries, through a shared expertise in teaching, is also important. Future faculty face challenges significantly different from those of their predecessors, including working with students who represent increasingly diverse ethnic and academic backgrounds (Gappa, Austin, and Trice, 2007). Further, data from the 2009 Council of Graduate Schools (CGS) and the Graduate Record Examinations (GRE) Survey of Graduate Enrollment and Degrees indicate that faculty responsibilities in assessment have increased, necessitating graduate student pedagogical training in assessment (Council of Graduate Schools, 2011). To succeed in future professions or academe, graduate students will need opportunities to engage with the scholarship of teaching, which is best gained through connections with peers and faculty to address topics such as how to develop and assess curriculum, foster diverse learning opportunities, and address classroom challenges.

One distinctive aspect of our learning community is the use of a wiki to structure mentoring communication and article drafting. With its opportunities for interaction, feedback cycles, and fluid mentoring roles, online collaboration can enrich traditional forms of professional development support and academic socialization. Initial studies on collaborative learning on the graduate level suggest that much-needed knowledge sharing, conversation, and reflection are well supported by tools like wikis (DiPietro and others, 2010). We have seen wikis operate as a place faculty and graduate students enter on relatively equal footing, a locus for practicing the peer review expected of future professors. We expect that graduate students who have had this positive experience sharing peer review on a wiki will be able to employ wikis in their own classrooms as GTAs and model the same style of professional communication with undergraduates online.

Workshops on Humor, Classroom Disruptions, and Boundaries

A teaching assistant receives a very informal e-mail from a student that reads: "Hey Dude. What's up? I'm that handsome kid that was sitting in the corner, with the red hat, remember me? Got a question for you. When is that paper about that thing we talked about in class due? Maaaannnn I'm being lazy these days (lol), you mind if I copy the paper from someone else? You know, no cheating or anything, he's my cousin so that doesn't count. Besides, you're an all cool TA, I'm sure you won't tell. Take care!"

An instructional intern composed this hypothetical e-mail to use as an example in a workshop discussion on classroom humor and its boundaries. As shocking as the tone and content of this e-mail might be, it is a composite of types of correspondence teaching assistants (even some faculty) report receiving routinely at the beginning of the semester. On the surface the response is obvious; the undergraduate will learn that the GTA will not overlook basic conduct rules. However, this kind of correspondence from undergraduates raises complex interpersonal issues, as the student writer seeks to relate to the instructor by paradoxically testing the boundaries of classroom dynamics. The subtle issue is how communication will be handled, as these kinds of early contacts establish classroom climate and affective learning dynamics (Mazer, Murphy, and Simonds, 2007). Workshop participants shared their written responses, which were professional in format but varied in tone. Most GTAs gravitated toward a formal response to model to the undergraduate how communication will need to be structured, which is one powerful way to reestablish power dynamics and remind students of their broader academic context.

This humor workshop is a specific example of our most common requests for classroom management support. These workshops invariably involve discussion about establishing boundaries and developing a teaching persona. In working with GTAs to facilitate workshops on these topics, we found recent scholarship on the topic a useful starting point, in particular, Valeri Helterbran's essay "The Ideal Professor" (2008). For instance, a positive quality, such as having a "good sense of humor," can also be negatively viewed as "embarrassing, made fun of my hometown." Contrasting students' positive and negative reactions and recognizing the sometimes arbitrary nature of these judgments enables an open discussion about teaching styles. Although we have presented a workshop on boundary issues ourselves, the preferred means of training is to work with the GTAs to present to their peers. This nuance can sometimes be frustrating if a GTA insists on right and wrong approaches. We work toward conveying that a teaching style and persona is a choice, and short of illegally harassing students or showing them disrespect, there are few rights or wrongs. GTAs come to recognize that one faculty member may appear in class looking like he's about to attend a Grateful Dead concert, use colorful language, disclose details of his personal life, and find this an effective teaching style; another may be more comfortable keeping his personal life private while wearing formal attire and using formal language. The key to any successful teaching persona is that it facilitates student learning.

High-impact workshops provide interactive exercises that enable GTAs to explore different approaches to decide what feels right and what facilitates learning in their classrooms. Role-playing and video vignettes can open discussion about how to handle minor classroom disruptions that are the result of boundaries being crossed. Other sessions have addressed how to manage classroom discussion, with self-disclosure considerations about the extent to which an instructor would want to interpose a religious, cultural, or political viewpoint during discussion. San Francisco State University, for example, several years ago created a series of very short videos of classroom situations, sometimes humorous, that allow GTAs to discuss possible reactions to cell phone interruptions, heated discussions, and grade disputes (Casella and Kelly, 2003). These kinds of professional development tools and practices facilitate engaged workshop discussion about the benefits and challenges of self-disclosure, particularly in small classroom settings.

Communicating Productivity: Boundaries Between Grad Students and Faculty Mentors

A professor and grad student discuss how the student's time is spent. The professor jokes about the graduate student's enjoyment of pulp fiction and reality television. When the graduate student mentions an upcoming holiday with his family, the professor responds cryptically: "Serious academics read journals and stay in the office over holidays. How do you expect to succeed?"

The graduate student reaction to this type of conversation can be indignation: "How dare the professor tell me what to do with my time!" An interpersonal boundary has been crossed. Although no one seriously expects scholars to abandon all hope of a personal life, there is a grain of truth to the notion that faculty workload is significant. Workload has increased appreciably in the past two decades (National Center for Education Statistics, 2010) in the areas of research, teaching, and service and also with administrative tasks, professional development activities, and assessment. Graduate students frequently report not fully understanding professional demands and employment pressures until several years into a program. For example, Golde and Dore's longitudinal graduate survey analysis (2001) found two key conclusions: "The training doctoral students receive is not what they want, nor does it prepare them for the jobs they take. Many students do not clearly understand what doctoral study entails, how the process works, and how to navigate it effectively" (p. 5). Graduate students must learn to negotiate the realities of a profession that challenges traditional nine-to-five boundaries of work and personal life. Simultaneously, faculty advisers need to respect personal boundaries as they counsel graduate students about professional success benchmarks and productivity. This balancing of personal and research time is complicated by a need at many universities for graduate students to fund their studies through teaching assistantships. Without a clear means for communicating research productivity with mentors, graduate students can find themselves in a complex set of workload negotiations.

Historically, doctoral programs struggled with high attrition rates and long times to degree, particularly in the humanities and social sciences. Anticipated graduation degree times average at six years; however, only 50 percent of humanities and social science graduate students complete degrees within eight years (Ehrenberg, Zuckerman, Groen, and Brucker, 2010). The probability of being in a tenure-track position three years after degree receipt declines with time to degree for those who took eight years or more to complete the degrees (Groen, 2008; Ehrenberg, Zuckerman, Groen, and Brucker, 2010). Comprehensive national studies like the Graduate Education Initiative (1991–2001), funded by an $85 million Andrew W. Mellon foundation grant, have demonstrated the significance of faculty mentoring on time-to-degree factors. Establishing professional boundaries between mentors and advisees involves effective communication regarding productivity. Improving this communication may be among the keys to strengthening graduate student persistence and time to degree, in that it creates benchmarks and structures expectations.

How graduate students communicate productivity is discipline and person specific, which makes this a difficult skill to teach. In addition, in an era when research can take place outside a library or lab via the Internet, productivity is less likely to be reflected by time on campus. With work less visible, interpersonal conflicts with senior faculty are more likely to occur. To help graduate students avoid this type of conflict, we held a workshop featuring strategies and tools to better communicate graduate student productivity. Led by two assistant professors, the workshop acknowledged the perils of poor communication between faculty mentors and graduate students. It focused on formal and informal means for communicating research goals. The learning outcomes expected participants to (1) identify goals and potential obstacles on the way to degree completion, (2) establish important characteristics of a high-quality PhD, and (3) explore some planning and communication strategies that reduce obstacles to goals. This workshop provided checklists and workload reporting forms as a communications framework; graduate students also gained a clear understanding of two professors' expectations and approaches to productivity. One faculty member's approach was structured weekly progress reports; another approach was open ended and specific to long-term research outcomes, for example, a section to a grant or technical paper. Both faculty members took a timeline-to-degree approach to communicating productivity that privileges explicit mentoring expectations and emphasizes field-specific standards, which may minimize personal conflicts. Because each professor exhibited slightly different expectations and styles, the workshop underscored the importance of explicit conversations with advisers about workload and the boundaries between personal and work life. The relationship between faculty mentors and graduate students in some ways mirrors the relationship between GTAs and undergraduate students. A learning outcome approach to undergraduate instruction, as modeled through these mentoring practices, illustrates clear expectations and can reduce interpersonal conflicts between GTAs and their students.

Conclusion

In his week-by-week guide for college teachers, Lang (2008) cautions new instructors against thinking of themselves as peers or friends of students (see chapter 15 in particular). He notes, "The kind of relationship you want to forge with your students and what kind of teaching persona you want to construct is a complex one" (p. 23). In providing pedagogical training for a new and growing research university, we have discovered that GTAs confront boundary issues beyond the classroom with undergraduates, including important negotiations with peers and faculty that contribute toward a professional identity. Further, every aspect of our training for GTAs deals with boundaries in some fashion, and helping graduate students make intentional choices about those boundaries is an essential element of professional development. In the end, we expect that GTAs who have paid attention to establishing professional boundaries with students, with colleagues, and with their personal lives will be more confident and successful in their self-presentation and therefore more effective instructors and more employable (Meizlish and Kaplan, 2008). A strong sense of professional identity is an important asset in what one author has described as "the changing world of employment for PhDs . . . that necessarily . . . requires graduates to develop a philosophy about scholarship, education, and leadership; accommodate diversity; and understand how to continue to learn and adapt to changing situations" (Austin, 2002, p.101).

References

Allitt, P. *I'm the Teacher, You're the Student: A Semester in the University Classroom.* Philadelphia: University of Pennsylvania Press, 2005.

Austin, A. "Preparing the Next Generation of Faculty: Graduate School as Socialization to the Academic Career." *Journal of Higher Education,* 2002, 73(1), 94–122.

Casella, V., and Kelly, K. "Classroom Management." San Francisco State University, Center for the Enhancement of Teaching, teaching module, http://oct.sfsu.edu /implementation/management/index.html, 2003.

NEW DIRECTIONS FOR TEACHING AND LEARNING • DOI: 10.1002/tl

Council of Graduate Schools. "Preparing Future Faculty to Assess Student Learning." Washington, D.C.: Council of Graduate Schools, 2011.

DiPietro, J., and others. "Using Wikis to Collaboratively Prepare for Qualifying Exams." *TechTrends,* 2010, *54*(1), 25–32.

Ehrenberg, R., Zuckerman, H., Groen, J., and Brucker, S. *Educating Scholars: Doctoral Education in the Humanities.* Princeton, N.J.: Princeton University Press, 2010.

Gappa, J., Austin, A., and Trice, A. *Rethinking Faculty Work: Higher Education's Strategic Imperative.* Hoboken, N.J.: John Wiley & Sons, 2007.

Gibbs, G., & Coffey, M. "Training to Teach in Higher Education: A Research Agenda." *Teacher Development,* 2000, *4*(1), 31–44.

Golde, C., and Dore, T. *At Cross Purposes: What the Experiences of Today's Doctoral Students Reveal about Doctoral Education.* Philadelphia: Pew Charitable Trusts, 2001.

Gorham, J., Cohen, S., and Morris, T. "Fashion in the Classroom III: Effects of Instructor Attire and Immediacy on Natural Classroom Interactions." *Communication Quarterly,* 1999, *47*(3), 281–299.

Groen, J. "Program Design and Student Outcomes in Graduate Education." *Economics of Education Review,* 2008, *27*(2), 111–124.

Helterbran, V. "The Ideal Professor: Student Perceptions of Effective Instructor Practices, Attitudes, and Skills." *Education,* 2008, *129*(1), 125–138.

Lang, J. *On Course: A Week-by-Week Guide to Your First Semester of College Teaching.* Cambridge, Mass.: Harvard University Press, 2008.

Lovitts, B. *Leaving the Ivory Tower: The Causes and Consequences of Departure from Doctoral Study.* Lanham, Md.: Rowman & Littlefield, 2001.

Mazer, J. P., Murphy, R. E., and Simonds, C. J. "I'll See You on *Facebook*: The Effects of Computer-Mediated Teacher Self-Disclosure on Student Motivation, Affective Learning, and Classroom Climate." *Communication Education,* 2007, *56*(1), 1–17.

Mazer, J. P., Murphy, R. E. and Simonds, C. J. "The Effects of Teacher Self-Disclosure Via *Facebook* on Teacher Credibility." *Learning, Media, and Technology,* 2009, *34*(2),175–183.

Meizlish, D., and Kaplan, M. "Valuing and Evaluating Teaching in Academic Hiring: A Multidisciplinary, Cross-Institutional Study." *Journal of Higher Education,* 2008, *79*(5), 489–512.

National Center for Education Statistics. Mini-Digest of Education Statistics 2009. "Table 255. Employees in Degree-Granting Institutions, by Primary Occupation." Washington, D.C.: Institute for Education Sciences, 2010.

O'Neal, C., and others. "The Impact of Teaching Assistants on Student Retention in the Sciences." *Journal of College Science Teaching,* 2007, *36*(5), 24–29.

Parini, J. *The Art of Teaching.* London: Oxford University Press, 2004.

Pascarella, E., and Terenzi, P. *How College Affects Students: Findings and Insights from Twenty Years of Research.* San Francisco: Jossey-Bass, 1991.

Prieto, L., and Altmaier, E. "The Relationship of Prior Training and Previous Teaching Experience to Self-Efficacy Among Graduate Teaching Assistants." *Research in Higher Education,* 1994, *35*(4), 481–497.

Rice, K., and others. "International Student Perspectives on Graduate Advising Relationships." *Journal of Counseling Psychology,* 2009, *56*(3), 376–391.

Roach, D. "Effects of Graduate Teaching Assistant Attire on Student Learning, Misbehaviors, and Ratings of Instruction." *Communication Quarterly,* 1997, *45*(3),125–141.

Robertson, C., Dyer, C., and Campbell, D. "Campus Harassment: Sexual Harassment Policies and Procedures at Institutions of Higher Learning." *Signs: Journal of Women in Culture and Society,* 1988, *13*(4), 792–812.

Stigler, J. W., and Hiebert, J. *The Teaching Gap.* New York: Free Press, 1999.

Tinto, V. "Classrooms as Communities: Exploring the Educational Character of Student Persistence." *Journal of Higher Education,* 1997, 68(6), 599–623.

KAREN DUNN-HALEY, PhD, is the faculty development and accreditation coordinator, Center for Research on Teaching Excellence, University of California, Merced.

ANNE ZANZUCCHI, PhD, is the associate director of the writing program and assessment coordinator, Center for Research on Teaching Excellence, University of California, Merced.

7

This chapter explores the critical nature of relational learning and boundary crossing in a doctoral program that combines low-residency and community online learning.

Crossing Boundaries in Doctoral Education: Relational Learning, Cohort Communities, and Dissertation Committees

Elizabeth L. Holloway, Laurien Alexandre

This chapter explores relational boundary crossing in doctoral education as a way to improve student learning and faculty satisfaction. A brief introduction sets the stage by articulating a recognized set of challenges for student learning in the current context of U.S. doctoral education. The chapter then introduces elements of an innovative twenty-first century doctoral study with a focus on a successful interdisciplinary doctoral program in which both authors have worked for over a decade. In particular, the authors explore key aspects of program design, including the nature of relational learning in cohort communities of practitioner-scholars as well as the nature of relational practice among faculty members with a specific focus on the culminating dissertation committees. Evidence demonstrates that a primary focus on student learning that incorporates intentional relational practice has increased student persistence and graduation and enriched faculty work lives.

Both authors have been involved in the design and development of a distinctive geographically dispersed low-residency doctoral program in leadership and change for the past decade. The program includes students from across the United States as well as abroad who meet four times a year at various Antioch campuses for residencies and otherwise pursue their

NEW DIRECTIONS FOR TEACHING AND LEARNING, no. 131, Fall 2012 © Wiley Periodicals, Inc.
Published online in Wiley Online Library (wileyonlinelibrary.com) • DOI: 10.1002/tl.20029

studies using a variety of technologies to stay connected with their cohort and faculty. This effort has challenged, humbled, and inspired us. We have discovered the complexity of navigating across multiple boundaries of teaching and learning in the paradoxical context of intensive face-to-face quarterly residencies combined with at-a-distance, technologically enabled, interresidency periods.

The authors' roles have differed—one is a full-time faculty member and the other is a program director with some advising and teaching responsibilities. Holloway's background is in counseling psychology, and she has spent many years teaching in traditional doctoral programs and practicing in clinical work while researching supervisory discourse and respectful engagement in the workplace. Her work has been built on relationship development as a vehicle for change. Alexandre's background is as an interdisciplinary social scientist with expertise in media and gender studies. For the past two decades, she has served as an academic administrator with a keen interest in relational leadership.

Challenges to Student Success in U.S. Doctoral Education

Despite its many successes, U.S. doctoral education is replete with disturbing characteristics and outcomes. Findings show that most recipients are inadequately prepared for the settings in which they will work; women and ethnic minorities are underrepresented, attrition often exceeds 50 percent with higher numbers in the humanities and social sciences (slightly lower in the fields of science, technology, engineering, and mathematics), and program time to completion is now well over seven and a half to eight years (Council of Graduate Schools, 2006). Any other system with such disgraceful results would be in need of a major overhaul instead of, as often is the case in doctoral study, declared indicators of quality because those who don't graduate simply don't have the intellectual capacity.

In *Leaving the Ivory Tower*, Lovitts (2001) suggests that it is not students' background characteristics that affect their persistence outcomes but what happens to them after they arrive at the university. She notes the isolation, chilly climate, lack of access to faculty, and peer competition as contributing to students' experiences of inadequacy and distaste for academic life.

We believe that many of these negative characteristics can be addressed effectively by the intentional inclusion of relational practices in the ways students and faculty interact with and empower each other. Lovitts's recommendations for changing the organizational culture and social structure of graduate education to promote student retention, research relevance, and nurturing learning communities support this position. The calls for these types of structural shifts are part of a more generalized call for rethinking the PhD to meet the demands of the twenty-first century.

NEW DIRECTIONS FOR TEACHING AND LEARNING • DOI: 10.1002/tl

Unfortunately, while we see a rise of new forms of interdisciplinary and practice-based doctoral study (Boud and Lee, 2009), many programs replicate the unproductive aspects of traditional doctoral culture and have given scant attention to the changing demographics and needs of doctoral students as adult learners. For example, traditional doctoral programs have not shifted to the twenty-first century student learners who are older, working adults reflecting diversity in gender, race, ethnicity, class, and international cultures (Kasworm and Bowles, 2010). Kasworm and Bowles argue that "remaking" doctoral education to "fit" today's students requires a focus on self-directed learners, an understanding of the impact of forming and re-forming social and personal identities through transformative learning, and the significance of multiple and diverse communities of practice as an influence on student learning. To focus on high-achieving professional adult self-directed students changes the nature of student-to-student and student-to-faculty relational power structures. Adult students bring life experiences that draw into question traditional notions of expertise. Holders of rank and authority outside the academy have the maturity to question authority relations inside the academy.

So what are characteristics of a doctoral program that can successfully attract and retain "new" doctoral students? How does relational learning recast doctoral faculty work?

Antioch's PhD in Leadership and Change

Originally founded by noted abolitionist Horace Mann in 1852, Antioch was in the forefront of combining academic study with nonacademic work in the 1920s. Continuing this tradition, in the 1960s, Antioch experimented with interdisciplinary teaching and learning, student-centered education, egalitarianism in classroom and governance, experiential learning, and a focus on teaching rather than on research (Kliewer, 2001).

Confident in its historic distinctiveness, Antioch University inaugurated an interdisciplinary PhD in Leadership and Change in 2002. The program was highly innovative in design and delivery, framed in Antioch's historic mission valuing the interconnectivity of theory and practice, a deep commitment to social justice, and grounded in well-established research on adult learning. The program is a cohort-based, outcomes-based, geographically dispersed doctoral program designed for experienced professionals who are leading change in their respective fields of practice. A recent ten-year external program review concluded that the program "is serving as a national model to inform the continuing discussion of the nature of doctoral education in the United States and around the world" (Eby and Plater, 2010, p. 4).

With its "blended" learning design, the program holds quarterly residencies attended by all faculty and students, who travel from across the nation and internationally to attend. These residencies raise many

NEW DIRECTIONS FOR TEACHING AND LEARNING • DOI: 10.1002/tl

relationally challenging considerations as faculty and students meet not only in classroom settings but also in restaurants and hotels and other non-program situations. As a learning community of over one hundred adult students and a dozen faculty travel away from home and work, appropriate professional behavior and boundaries are based on good judgment and a seasoned sense of self.

Interresidency periods raise a different set of relationally challenging considerations, as the learning community engages in robust technologically enabled forms of communication. In addition to phone, e-mail, and the structured processes of the program's Learning Management System, students and faculty now also incorporate Skype, Adobe Connect, Facebook, LinkedIn, and other social media. There is no official downtime; contact is virtually twenty-four hours a day, seven days a week, and the expectation of almost immediate response time continues to rise. The fact that faculty members work from home offices adds to the difficulty of establishing and retaining one's own private and separate space. Responding to these demands, we have established guidelines for faculty members and students to allow forty-eight hours for e-mail responses and two weeks for feedback on written work. As more students become engaged in social media networking sites, the faculty has discussed issues around being connected to students on such sites. Although it is an individual faculty member's decision, we, as a faculty, have not chosen to join the more personally oriented sites, but many of us have joined professional networking sites that include our current and former students. (For an in-depth consideration of boundaries in the context of social media, see Chapter Two of this sourcebook.)

With an interdisciplinary community of faculty and students, the curriculum is designed to provide a learner-centered structure for both peer and individual study with an emphasis on academic rigor, applied research, experiential learning, and reflective practice. Traditional "courses" have been replaced by structured and sequenced "learning achievements." Grades have been replaced by extensive narrative evaluations. The traditional dissertation has been retained and is discussed later in this chapter.

Each annual cohort of twenty-five to thirty students is a highly diverse group characterized by a mix of professional sectors. Typically each cohort has close to 65 percent women; approximately 50 percent of a cohort is in their fifties; and nearly 40 percent are persons of color. These are today's doctoral students!

Retention is much higher than traditional doctoral programs: nearly 75 percent of entering students earn their PhDs in seven years or less. We believe two factors account for this, factors that are deeply connected to the relational practices of the program. First, learning experiences are structured so that each builds on the others, thus generating a strong sense of momentum based on the student's passion and professional practice.

Second, the program relies on strong personal support among cohort members and with faculty.

The program design, coupled with this extraordinary diversity, promotes a level of collaborative learning that is rare in doctoral education. The embeddedness of relational community building allays the geographical distance and addresses many of the challenges mentioned earlier in this chapter.

Creating Communities of Relational Learning Across Difference

To support student success, we believe it is necessary to create communities of mutually beneficial and respectful learning as opposed to programs based on peer competition and isolation. As noted by Ehrenberg and Kuh (2009) in *Doctoral Education and the Faculty of the Future*, efforts to improve doctoral education should focus on the characteristics of the curriculum, the advising provided to students, clearly articulating objectives and requirements, and integrating faculty and students into a community of scholars.

Taking a holistic approach to rethinking doctoral study means that in addition to redressing curricula and pedagogy, we believe there is something essential about establishing a welcoming community that honors each individual into a culture of high individuality and equal worth. This is at the core of Antioch's program culture. This approach doesn't naively assume that all participants are the same. Clearly, individual students are more or less prepared for intense advanced study, more or less engaged in learning, and the like. There are obviously authority differences and positional power relationships. Faculty must evaluate students' work and the degree to which standards of rigor and competence have been met. Yet, all this said, people within this learning community come together as equals although having different roles and responsibilities.

Much emphasis is placed on learning effectively together and creating a shared community identity. It is not an afterthought. The program intentionally places emphasis on "relational practice," as discussed by Fletcher (2001), in terms of trust, mutuality, and empathy, not characteristics traditionally associated with doctoral study. The program is committed to the underlying belief that each and every community member has the ability and the right to succeed. That message is reiterated in many ways. The norms for respectful discourse—listening, reflecting, valuing—are set forth from the first day forward. Behaviors that reinforce shared knowledge building and peer learning are valued. This is particularly important in a doctoral community that is as highly diverse as ours. In discussing the ways in which the program's learning environment enables difficult topics, such as marginalization and inclusion, to be discussed and mutual learning to be practiced, one student noted, "As a member of a particular cohort and of the larger doctoral community, I feel I must take responsibility for

NEW DIRECTIONS FOR TEACHING AND LEARNING • DOI: 10.1002/tl

creating a welcoming and safe environment. Creating a welcoming environment is a shared effort." Another student noted, "The faculty and students have worked effectively to create a sense of community and reasonable trust, both of which are critical in developing a safe learning space." This sense of personal trust and safety assumes that community members feel comfortable to self-disclose and share a level of intimacy that requires relational comfort, a common ground that is often hard to find in the deeply divided and polarized culture of the United States.

The program takes seriously welcoming the whole person in other rather unique forms as well. For example, the program invites partners and spouses to all residencies and has created a "partners' track" (special residency sessions designed for significant others). And graduates are invited back to residencies anytime, as this becomes their lifelong learning community. These decisions ask all members of the community to be open to different "status" of learners and move within the boundaries of their own roles without violating the trust of others. We believe creating an open relational community of mutuality and respectful engagement across differences of role and status greatly enhances students' self-awareness as leaders and change agents.

Faculty: From Self to Team Focused

Maintaining a learning community that values the sorts of relational practices in faculty–student relations discussed earlier requires significant attention to the structure and quality of faculty–faculty relations. The program has established intentional and strategic ways to build relational bonds among the dozen faculty members. After an initial discussion, we examine how this manifests in the culminating experience of the dissertation and faculty relations on the dissertation committee.

Faculty with Faculty. Whereas traditional doctoral faculty members focus on their own research and the all-powerful one-on-one apprenticeship of advanced students, Antioch's PhD faculty members place primacy on student success, with learners being supported by a proactive interdisciplinary faculty team. In support of that, the program has established intentional structures that value, require, and reward faculty collaboration. For example, we jointly create the residency schedules and engage in extensive team teaching. To the degree possible and appropriate, we rotate responsibility for sessions so that no one "course" belongs to an individual faculty member. Two faculty members evaluate every student assignment, which requires a sense of trust among the faculty members that another is not judging their professionalism or competence. Rather, one faculty member focuses on the student's demonstration of the required learning goals or the particular assignment and the other focuses on the student's development over time across many assignments.

NEW DIRECTIONS FOR TEACHING AND LEARNING • DOI: 10.1002/tl

There is another important way in which the program creates the conditions for relations of trust, equality, and collaboration. Antioch University does not have tenure, but the PhD program does have a rank process, and all program faculty members hold the same senior rank—full professor—and receive the same salary. This eliminates a caste system that rewards through monetary or other means the contributions of one member as more important than another. It also eliminates some of the pain and difficulty of peers in a small unit making promotion decisions. The annual performance reviews take into account and recognize the faculty members' collaborative orientation and contribution to the team. Faculty members are mutually dependent on each other to achieve our individual and collective purposes, which are student success and program excellence. When faculty members act outside of this norm, the disruption is apparent. For example, when a faculty member assumes the sort of one-on-one apprenticeship or ownership of a student, it causes friction within the faculty body, isolates the student (albeit she or he may not realize that), and causes abnormalities in our program's relational efforts.

Overall, faculty members consider the connectivity and team spirit to be one of the strengths of the program and one of the most satisfying aspects of their work lives. In all surveys of faculty satisfaction completed for program self-studies, faculty members express a high degree of satisfaction with the way they work together in a noncompetitive environment that honors what each contributes. Fostering this sort of faculty team feels like it comes naturally but, in fact, as discussed, the program is intentional in establishing ways in which the relational practice of faculty members is nurtured in this interdisciplinary team.

Crossing Relational Boundaries on the Road to the Dissertation

All of this boundary-crossing relational practice for student success comes to a culmination in the dissertation process, a component of doctoral study that is often fraught with ego-driven tension and discipline-reified conflict that too often damages students.

Despite or perhaps because of the program's innovative nature, the decision was made to require a traditional dissertation. One reason is, frankly, pragmatic, as a PhD program that did not require a dissertation would lack academic credibility. The PhD is by definition a research degree, and its holders are expected to enrich the knowledge base of their disciplines or professions.

The primary focus of what has been written about the supervision and mentorship of the doctoral student examines the centrality of the dissertation chair–adviser and doctoral candidate. Other dissertation committee members typically remain in the shadowed background of the student's journey. Furthermore, it is typically assumed that the doctoral student enters a program with an adviser who will most likely become the chair of the dissertation; if not, the student will transfer to the prospective chair early in his or her program of study. Yet the singular focus on one individual faculty member is inconsistent with our program model and potentially detrimental to student success.

Based on its study of eighty-four doctoral departments from forty-four universities, the Carnegie Initiative on the Doctorate noted the signature pedagogy of doctoral education—apprenticeship—but argued that it not be done in isolation, for a "healthy and vibrant intellectual community provides the best environment for effective graduate education" and that such a community can be created deliberately. The authors propose a "shift of prepositions: from a system in which students are apprenticed *to* a single faculty mentor to one in which they apprentice *with* several mentors" (Golde, Bueschel, Jones, and Walker, 2006, p. 53). Their reframed mode of apprenticeship has four features:

1. *Intentional pedagogy.* Mentors as expert practitioners engage students in repetitive practice with coaching and feedback and structured support.
2. *Multiple relationships.* Students have formal mentors who guide their development in research and teaching as well as less formal mentoring relationships.
3. *Collective responsibility.* Mentors work collaboratively from a shared vision of student development.
4. *Apprenticeship with* (versus apprenticeship *to*). Mentors seek to develop relationships of mutual respect, based on trust that grows over time through quality interactions. These are reciprocal relationships wherein both sides gain—student gets training, advice, sponsorship, support, feedback; faculty member gets new ideas, infusion of energy, satisfaction.

As is by now apparent, the shift in power differential between apprentice and mentor is radically different from the singular faculty mentor model. In this nested apprenticeship model, students are empowered to choose whose expertise and style best fits their learning needs during different stages along the path to the dissertation. Such shared mentoring requires faculty members to work collaboratively rather than possessively with students in an open and flexible space of distributed relational connections. It is easy for faculty members to experience greater vulnerability and threat without the traditional structure of singular power "over." However, there are common features between distributed apprenticeship models, creation of thriving intellectual communities, and the growing research on positive relationships. Particularly relevant to intellectual functioning are the relationships between good feelings (that is, positive emotions, moods, and sentiments) and widened scope of attention, broadened behavioral repertoires, and increased intuition and creativity (Fredrickson and

Losada, 2005). Relationships with these characteristics can greatly contribute to a student's successful completion of the dissertation work.

Despite the obvious benefits of distributed apprenticeship, which decreases the hierarchies between faculty and students, there are opportunities for much role confusion when faculty members inadvertently relinquish too much of their positionality and power. Our program has experienced the damage when faculty members cross a relational boundary that conflicts with their primary role as educator and mentor. Consequently, our faculty members discuss openly the complexity of holding to a principle of "power with" the student while simultaneously maintaining the distance needed to evaluate the work (Buck, Mast, Macintyre, and Kaftan, 2009). For example, our feedback to students often takes the form of engaging their particular expertise in practice to lead them to the scholarly literature and voice needed in their work. In this way, students join us in improving the work not by merely incorporating our expertise but by strengthening the paper with their own tacit knowledge and practice wisdom. The result is a mutual sharing of expertise, that is, a "power with" relational engagement.

As described earlier, we have deliberately created a process that maximizes meaningful relational connections among students and multiple faculty members throughout their studies up to and including the dissertation. Thus, there are a number of significant relationships that influence the student and his or her scholarship throughout the program. Moving away from an essentially privatized relationship between a supervisor and student to our "distributed" practices of pedagogy and learning within a community of scholarly practice represents the shift that Boud and Lee (2009) applaud in doctoral programs. It is "a shift from the organizing idea of postgraduate research, which attended primarily to the production of research outputs, to the activities and relationships involved in doing doctoral work and producing doctoral graduates" (p. 1). Individual faculty members experience the ebb and flow of involvement with a student over time as other faculty members enter to pick up substantive areas of learning and support. Openly discussing shifts of involvement with students is critical in co-creating a relational context in which explicit expectations around roles and boundaries are clarified up front. Petty jealousies and ownership of one's "own" student have no place in this model.

Dissertation Committee. It is from this relational network that the dissertation committee emerges. The four-member committee typically is composed of the three-person internal working group, including the student's adviser, the mentor, and the chair (who may or may not have been the student's adviser); and the fourth member, the external reader. The members' relationships with the student and the chair are varied and much more complex than those among the typical dissertation committee members in traditional settings. Rather than being aligned only with the chair, the student will likely have deep and lasting relationships with all internal members of the committee. At the opposite end is the external reader who represents the traditional arm's-length member who has no relationship with the student other than reading the dissertation proposal and final report. The dissertation committee is an assemblage of persons who have been an integral part of the student's study of the dissertation topic. One might quickly conclude that such a committee has "too many irons in the fire" and a nightmare of management for the chair and student. The spheres of influence widen considerably when involvement with the student is both historical and substantive. All members of the committee are required to shift and adapt their traditional perception of their role and influence.

Another aspect of difference comes from the interdisciplinary nature of the program and the committee. In more traditional doctoral programs, a chair has the confidence of guiding students through familiar disciplinary terrain. Within a defined field of practice, we are members of a relatively small community of scholars who form networks of knowledge, debate, and influence. Although we may be competitive or disagree with others in our field, we know who they are, their scholarly lineage, and the foundation of their work. Our research is firmly anchored to historical and contemporary research in the field, and this ongoing knowledge of which we are a part allows us to guide our students in gaining access and privilege in the scholarly community. These are assumptions we make that form the foundation of the "expert" role in the mentoring and supervisory relationship. Our knowledge base and connection to a specific academic community is often the primary reason that a student chooses a dissertation chair, and a student's interest in a field of interest plays a role in the chair's decision to work with a student.

These traditional paths for the chair and student are less obvious in Antioch's interdisciplinary program. The chair will have a knowledge and practice in leadership and change, but it may be grounded in a field quite different from the student's area of interest. For example, just within the past year, we have chaired dissertations on organizational crisis, municipal communities of practice, nurse leadership, women social justice activists, social entrepreneurship, and Appalachian women's self-leadership, just to identify six of our more than seventy dissertations. They are all based on foundational knowledge in very different scholarly fields ranging from health care, to business, to cultural anthropology, to sociology. As mature learners and leaders in their respective fields, our students bring a wealth of experiential information and contemporary best practices knowledge to the subject area. Thus, in some ways, we find that the "expert" knowledge and connection to the field of knowledge and scholarship takes on a very different form.

Rather than the chair being the in-residence expert on the subject matter, students seek a mentor outside the program to guide their substantive inquiry into the scholarship of their topic. This content area mentor, once approved by the program, guides the student to ensure that the research question is relevant and meaningful to the specific scholarly literature in which the study will contribute. At this point, it is clear that there is a shared responsibility in guiding the student through the dissertation study and report around the substantive area of inquiry. The chair must depend on the mentor to guide the student to the specific area of scholarly discourse while simultaneously guiding him or her in the writing, editing, and protocol for the dissertation itself.

It is critically important that the chair remain primary in guiding the overall dissertation, but such guidance is influenced by the input of the content expert mentor. The mentor may be unfamiliar with the local protocols and implicit standards of quality of our program's dissertation. Thus, the chair is negotiating across the boundaries of the relationship with the student and the mentor, the student and self as chair, and the mentor and self as fellow committee member.

In such a morass of relationships (and we have only addressed the mentor committee member at this stage), let us now add a further complication to the network of relationships: the student's adviser. In their first year, students are encouraged to get to know all faculty members in the program so that before the second year, the students can select a faculty adviser. Students make this selection based on their perception of which faculty member will best help them navigate through the program. As they approach candidacy, students choose the dissertation chair, who may or may not have been the student's adviser. The student comes to the chair after careful consultation with the adviser on the best fit for methodology, supervisory style, or related content expertise and interest. The adviser typically serves on the dissertation committee; however, the chair is the primary guide of the student's dissertation work.

This structure for advising has been designed to enhance our collaborative and relational approach to student learning. It is a distributed influence model that in many ways flies in the face of traditional structures where students are "owned" by the "major professor" and are beholden to him or her for progress, recommendations, and, in some cases, even the topic for the research study. We want not only to maximize the opportunity for students to learn from and be guided by those faculty members who are best aligned with their professional and research interests but also to model the importance of collaboration among scholars with different fields of practice and scholarship.

This arrangement is not without its challenges at the time of the dissertation. The chair must carefully orchestrate a process that does not triangulate the student when there are different opinions. Although such differences are part of doing business in traditional committee structures, the long-term relationships students have with each member of the internal committee means differences or conflict among committee members often triangulate the student in a web of conflicting loyalties. Thus, the chair and committee members must have very clear boundaries around their roles on the committee and in relationship to guiding the student. Committee members must take up differences of opinion with the chair, who then negotiates among committee members. This approach avoids drawing students in and using the weight of prior relationship to sway them. These role boundaries are discussed openly among faculty members. At the beginning of the committee's formation, the chair articulates with the student the roles of each committee member. Even with such precautions, misunderstandings about the execution of the work can easily emerge. Such situations can be resolved without jeopardizing the student's progress only if there is a basis of relational trust, respect, and open communication among committee members. And to date, we have been successful.

As faculty members, we embark on this journey with our students knowing that, in this relationship, there is the potential for our own growth both intellectually and emotionally. Because of the interdisciplinary nature of our program, each student presents the opportunity to learn a new field of practice, a pioneering methodology, or an innovative application of known work. The relationship is not built on the power of our expertise that contributes to the student's interest; rather, it is built on the expertise of guiding relational learning in a way that successfully results in a well-executed and reported original study. As faculty members, we must remain centered and hold the relational tension among the often conflicting roles of ally, advocate, educator, mentor, and gatekeeper. This requires a delicate and firm hand in guiding the student through the intellectual and emotional demands of the dissertation work. A relational approach to this learning and teaching journey focuses on connecting the dissertator to chair and to the subject matter; knowing and knowledge are embedded in relationship (Buck, Mast, Macintyre, and Kaftan, 2009). The interstitial space of the relationship itself is a place where knowledge is mutually imparted and negotiated. As we have discovered in our living within a community of relational practice, it is a place of both risk and opportunity.

Conclusion

Embedding relational practice into the very fabric of our program's structure has been a challenging adventure. It flies in the face of boundaries relied on in traditional doctoral program structures yet appears to be at the core of addressing twenty-first-century educational models. It requires faculty members to work as a team for the common good of student learning and success; it requires students to engage in peer learning for mutual growth and not solely on individual attainment and competition; and it requires program leaders and faculty members to create different models of delivery and different expectations of student and faculty work, and to reward new ways of mutually engaged teaching and learning. For us, data on student persistence and graduation, and evidence of faculty satisfaction demonstrate that the challenge has been well worth the risks of navigating new relational structures in doctoral education.

References

Boud, D., and Lee, A. (eds.). *Changing Practices of Doctoral Education*. New York: Routledge, 2009.

Buck, G. A., Mast, C. M., Macintyre, M. A., and Kaftan J. M. "Fostering a Theoretical and Practical Understanding of Teaching as a Relational Process: A Feminist Participatory Study of Mentoring a Doctoral Student." *Educational Action Research,* 2009, *17*(4), 505–521.

Council of Graduate Schools. *Trends in graduate enrollment and degrees.* 2006. Retrieved from http://www.cgsnet.org/portals/0/pdf/DataSources_2006_01.pdf

Eby, K. K., and Plater, W. M. *External Review: PhD Program in Leadership and Change Antioch University*, unpublished document, May 30, 2010.

Ehrenberg, R. G., and Kuh, C. V. (eds.). *Doctoral Education and the Faculty of the Future.* Ithaca, N.Y.: Cornell University Press, 2009.

Fletcher, J. K. *Disappearing Acts: Gender, Power, and Relational Practice at Work.* Boston: MIT Press, 2001.

Fredrickson, B. L., and Losada, M. F. "Positive Affect and the Complex Dynamics of Human Flourishing." *American Psychologist,* 2005, *60*(7), 678–686.

Golde, C., Bueschel, A., Jones, L., and Walker, G. *Apprenticeship and Intellectual Community: Lessons from the Carnegie Initiative on the Doctorate.* Doctoral Education and the Faculty of the Future conference, Cornell University, Ithaca, New York, 2006.

Kasworm, C., and T. Bowles. "The Overlooked Significance of Doctoral Students as Adult Learners." In S. Gardner and P. Mendoza (eds.), *On Becoming a Scholar: Socialization and Development in Doctoral Education.* Sterling, Va.: Stylus Press, 2010.

Kliewer, J. R. "The Innovative Colleges and Universities of the 1960s and 1970s: Lessons from Six Alternative Institutions." In B. L. Smith and J. McCann (eds.), *Reinventing Ourselves: Interdisciplinary Education, Collaborative Learning and Experimentation in Higher Education.* Boston: Anker, 2001.

Lovitts, B. E. *Leaving the Ivory Tower: The Causes and Consequences of Departure from Doctoral Study.* Lanham, Md.: Rowman & Littlefield, 2001.

ELIZABETH L. HOLLOWAY *is professor of psychology in the leadership and change doctoral program of Antioch University.*

LAURIEN ALEXANDRE *is vice-chancellor at Antioch University and director of the leadership and change doctoral program.*

NEW DIRECTIONS FOR TEACHING AND LEARNING • DOI: 10.1002/tl

8

Setting, adjusting, and maintaining boundaries with students is a deeply reflective process that challenges us to consider and reconsider our assumptions and understandings of ourselves, our students, and our position as educators.

Reflection and Intention: Interpersonal Boundaries in Teaching and Learning

Harriet L. Schwartz

Prior to working on this sourcebook, I think that if asked, I would have responded that the essence of setting boundaries was in the moments *with* students—the moments when I clarify my availability or make the split-second decision about whether to self-disclose or not. After working with the contributing authors for this book and doing my own reflective work necessary to write for this volume, I have come to believe that while the moments with students are clearly important, the metacognitive journey before we even get to the student interaction is just as, if not more, important. As I reflect on the previous chapters and on how they have influenced my teaching practice, I have identified five themes: increase our awareness of power and positionality; examine reflexive boundaries; explore the assumptions we hold about our students; clarify expectations; and offer transparency.

Increase Our Awareness of Power and Positionality

Many of the authors in this book have pointed to the connections among power, position, and boundaries. This has pushed me to consider more deeply my power and position in the classroom. My experience on the last night of a recent course provides a good example. Students had finished their final presentations, and we were about ten minutes away from the scheduled end time of the class (9 P.M.). I wanted to solicit additional feedback from the students regarding the course structure, so I asked, "Does

NEW DIRECTIONS FOR TEACHING AND LEARNING, no. 131, Fall 2012 © Wiley Periodicals, Inc.
Published online in Wiley Online Library (wileyonlinelibrary.com) • DOI: 10.1002/tl.20030

anyone mind if we go a few minutes over tonight?" Just as the students indicated that they were fine with staying late, I realized that despite our good rapport, it would likely be difficult for any of them to say that they minded staying late. I realized that my gesture contradicted the reality of the power differential in the room.

Later in this chapter, I describe how I handled the situation. The point of this first part of the story is that the interplay between power and boundaries is complex. To act responsibly vis-à-vis boundaries and our positionality, we must fine-tune our awareness of the power dynamics in our teaching relationships.

Examine Reflexive Boundaries

As Dunn-Haley and Zanzucchi note in Chapter Six, many of us develop our teaching practices and personae based on how we were taught. Some of these conventions have shifted so dramatically in our culture that we cannot help but to change our approach, while other shifts still seem awkward or inappropriate. Most of us, in our undergraduate lives, would never have considered calling one of our professors at home on a weekend. Yet today students e-mail us anytime they have a question, twenty-four hours a day, seven days a week, and many of us answer e-mail late at night, early in the morning, and on weekends—e-mail correspondence without time boundaries has become the norm for many in higher education. The sharing of cell phone numbers may be less clear, however. A few years ago in a meeting, I mentioned that I share my cell phone number with my students. A colleague was disturbed by this. I explained that I teach adult students, some who can call only in the evening and that I no longer have a landline so my cell phone is the only option. I suspect that if I taught undergraduates who were available to meet during the day, I would be more reluctant to share my cell phone number.

Not all of these adjustments are technology related. In my first few years of teaching, I self-disclosed very little in the classroom. However, through my dissertation research, I realized that some students benefited from hearing their professors share stories of their own academic journey. This pushed me to reconsider my level of self-disclosure, and when I deem it appropriate, I am more forthcoming with my students. Similarly, in Chapter Seven, Holloway and Alexandre describe how faculty in an interdisciplinary doctoral program have had to reconsider their taken-for-granted interpersonal boundaries with each other as well as with students.

Although deeper reflection may lead us to shift some boundaries, we may hold fast to others. The point of examining reflexive boundaries is not always to alter them but to ensure that we are acting with clarity and intention.

Explore the Assumptions We Hold About Our Students

As we seek to know ourselves, we must also strive to consider the worldview from which our students are operating. The authors in this sourcebook remind us that students come from generational and cultural contexts that may be vastly different from our own and thus their very understanding of boundaries, relationship, and authority may also vary greatly. In Chapter Three, Espinoza notes that Millennial students are less likely to recognize the boundaries of authority and more likely to see the syllabus as negotiable than their predecessors. We could easily dismiss a student who asks for an alternative assignment, assuming that she respects neither the faculty position nor the sanctity of the syllabus. However, if we understand that this student's life experience with authority and with the written word is very different from our own, we might come to see this student as engaged rather than disrespectful. We still might not choose to alter the requirement, but by understanding the student's perspective, we can respond with respect rather than frustration.

Further, as educators, we may be quite clear regarding our boundaries and the learning culture we wish to create and yet some students will still be far more influenced by prior experience than by the boundaries we articulate. Yamashita and I suggest in Chapter Five that international students may hesitate to cross intercultural divides because they have had negative experiences with other professors in the past. In addition, Booth points out in Chapter One that students may have very little experience self-disclosing in the classroom or in written assignments and thus may be unclear as to what is appropriate. Reminding ourselves that students' understanding of boundaries may be vastly different from our own will help us to be more mindful as we seek to shape the interpersonal cultures of our classroom and online learning spaces.

Clarify Expectations

Several authors in this sourcebook encourage us to proactively clarify boundary expectations with students. In Chapter One, Booth suggests sharing clear guidelines with students regarding assignments and class activities that ask for self-disclosure. McEwan, writing about social media in Chapter Two, recommends that we clarify availability and intended response time. In Chapter Four, Booth and I propose engaging in explicit conversations with adult students regarding boundary questions such as accessibility, meeting locations, self-disclosure, and the collaborative process.

Offer Transparency

Finally, by acting with transparency, we can provide students with examples of our own thinking regarding the complexity of boundaries, position, and power. In the example noted earlier, when I asked my students if they minded staying late, I chose to share with them my immediate realization that while my intentions were good, I had put them in a difficult spot and that I wanted to rephrase my question in a way that I thought more accurately reflected the power differentials in the class. Instead of asking them if *it were okay* to stay late, I asked them *to* stay late and noted that anyone who had to leave on time should do so. I realize they still might have experienced some tension around what I was asking, given my position, but I felt that the question was more direct and honest. More important, I suspect, was that I provided a glimpse of my own struggle, which I hope modeled for them the ongoing quest to negotiate one's position power and wish to share power and the humanness of seeing a failed moment and trying to fix it.

Conclusion

From the first day of class when we introduce ourselves to our students to the day they graduate and friend us on Facebook, our lives as educators are filled with moments that require us to clarify and set boundaries. Our responses to these decision points indicate how we view both the line between our personal and professional lives and the nature of the teaching relationship. These moments reveal our awareness of power, position, and authority. Setting boundaries with students is, at its most effective, a deeply reflective process that challenges us to consider and reconsider our assumptions and understandings of ourselves, our students, and our position as educators. Moreover, by acting with intention and transparency, we help our students deepen their awareness of power and positionality, distance and connection. Through these moments, boundaries are not only about differentiation but also about the deeply connecting energy of authentic teaching relationships.

Harriet L. Schwartz, PhD, is an assistant professor in the School of Education at Carlow University in Pittsburgh.

New Directions for Teaching and Learning • DOI: 10.1002/tl

INDEX

TL128　**Evidence-Based Teaching**
William Buskist, James E. Groccia
What could be more important to college and university faculty than
teaching well? Indeed, the sheer output of empirical research on teaching
and learning and the number of journals and professional conferences
devoted to improving teaching reflects higher education's burgeoning
emphasis on preparing its teachers to do their jobs more effectively. In
the past several years researchers have not only investigated key variables
influencing teaching and learning, they also have applied empirical findings
to develop and refine new systems of teaching and learning—approaches
that provide the infrastructure for the day-to-day organization and
assessment of student learning over the course of an academic term. This
volume of *New Directions for Teaching and Learning* provides an overview
of these systems and offers an assessment of the effectiveness of each
relative to both student learning and enjoyment of the learning process.
The contributors are leading teaching scholars who have been responsible
for much of the research, theory, and application of these systems to college
and university teaching. These systems include the lecture, problem-based
learning, case studies, team-based learning, interteaching, service-learning,
just-in-time teaching, Web-based computer-aided personalized instruction,
and online teaching. Each contributor outlines the basic principles of a
system, describes how to implement the system, and reviews the empirical
research literature with respect to the system's overall effectiveness in
producing student learning and enhancing student enjoyment of the learning
process.
ISBN: 978-11181-80686

TL127　**Faculty and First-Generation College Students: Bridging the Classroom
Gap Together**
Vickie L. Harvey, Teresa Heinz Housel
The population of first-generation college students (FGS) is increasing in an
ever-tightening economy, a time when employers demand a college degree
even for an initial interview. According to a 2007 study by UCLA's Higher
Education Research Institute, nearly one in six freshmen at American four-
year institutions is first-generation. However, FGS often straddle different
cultures between school and home, and many feel socially, ethnically,
academically, and emotionally marginalized on campus. Because of these
disparities, FGS frequently encounter barriers to academic success and
require additional campus support resources. Some institutions offer
increased financial aid and loan-free aid packages to FGS, but these
remedies—although welcome—do not fully address the diverse and complex
challenges that these students experience.
　　Responding to these complexities, this volume's chapters extend previous
research by examining the multiple transitions experienced by both
undergraduate and graduate FGS. This volume's cutting-edge research will
help college and university administrators, faculty, and staff work better with
FGS through more effective pedagogy and institutional programs. Ultimately,
this volume affirms how learning communities are strengthened when they
include diverse student populations such as FGS and meet their particular
emotional, academic, and financial needs.
ISBN: 978-11181-42141

TL126   **Self-Regulated Learning**
Héfer Bembenutty
This volume reports new findings associating students' self-regulation
of learning with their academic achievement, motivation for learning,
and use of cognitive and learning strategies. Self-regulation of learning
is a hallmark of students' ability to remain goal-oriented while pursuing
academic-specific intentions in postsecondary education. Protecting such
long-term and temporally distant goals requires that college and university
students be proactive in directing their learning experiences, guide their own
behavior, seek help from appropriate sources, sustain motivation, and delay
gratification. The authors suggest how college students can control their
cognition and behavior to attain academic goals, select appropriate learning
strategies, and monitor and evaluate their academic progress.
　　This volume calls the attention of students and educators to the vital
role that self-regulation plays in every aspect of postsecondary education.
The contributors provide compelling evidence supporting the notion that
self-regulation is related to positive academic outcomes, such as delay of
gratification, self-efficacy beliefs, and use of cognitive strategies, and that it is
important for the training of teachers and school psychologists. The authors
offer diverse vantage points from which students, teachers, administrators,
and policy makers can orchestrate their efforts to empower students with
self-regulatory learning strategies, appropriate motivational beliefs, and
academic knowledge and skills.
ISBN: 978-11180-91630

TL125   **An Integrative Analysis Approach to Diversity in the College Classroom**
Mathew L. Ouellett
College and university instructors continue to seek models that help
students to better understand today's complex social relationships. Feminist,
Queer, and Ethnic Studies scholars put forward compelling arguments for
more integrative understandings of race, class, gender, and sexuality and for
centering the experiences of women, people of color, and others traditionally
relegated to the margins. Intersectionality is one such approach.
　　In nine chapters, the contributors to this volume offer an overview of
key tenets of intersectionality and explore applications of this model in
faculty and instructional development in higher education. Gathered from
across the disciplines, they draw upon a range of approaches to social
identity formation, different theoretical models, and a complement of lived
experiences. When read together, these chapters offer a systemic approach to
change in higher education by addressing innovations at course, department,
and institutional levels.
　　Intersectionality does not advocate for a flattening of differences. Instead,
it argues for another layer of critical analyses that acknowledge the powerful
interplay of the many aspects of social identity to address the rapidly shifting
ways in which we talk about and describe identities in society and the
complexity of classroom dynamics in the academy today. By illuminating
the interconnected nature of systems of oppression, we shine a light on the
potential for disrupting the status quo and create stronger alliances for social
justice.
ISBN: 978-11180-27622

NEW DIRECTIONS FOR TEACHING AND LEARNING

ORDER FORM SUBSCRIPTION AND SINGLE ISSUES

DISCOUNTED BACK ISSUES:

Use this form to receive 20% off all back issues of *New Directions for Teaching and Learning*.
All single issues priced at **$23.20** (normally $29.00)

TITLE   ISSUE NO.   ISBN

_____   _____   _____

_____   _____   _____

_____   _____   _____

Call 888-378-2537 or see mailing instructions below. When calling, mention the promotional code JBNND
to receive your discount. For a complete list of issues, please visit www.josseybass.com/go/ndtl

SUBSCRIPTIONS: (1 YEAR, 4 ISSUES)

☐ New Order   ☐ Renewal

U.S.	☐ Individual: $89	☐ Institutional: $275
CANADA/MEXICO	☐ Individual: $89	☐ Institutional: $315
ALL OTHERS	☐ Individual: $113	☐ Institutional: $349

Call 888-378-2537 or see mailing and pricing instructions below.
Online subscriptions are available at www.onlinelibrary.wiley.com

ORDER TOTALS:

Issue / Subscription Amount: $ _____

Shipping Amount: $ _____
(for single issues only – subscription prices include shipping)

Total Amount: $ _____

SHIPPING CHARGES:

First Item $6.00
Each Add'l Item $2.00

*(No sales tax for U.S. subscriptions. Canadian residents, add GST for subscription orders. Individual rate subscriptions must
be paid by personal check or credit card. Individual rate subscriptions may not be resold as library copies.)*

BILLING & SHIPPING INFORMATION:

☐ **PAYMENT ENCLOSED:** *(U.S. check or money order only. All payments must be in U.S. dollars.)*

☐ **CREDIT CARD:**   ☐VISA   ☐MC   ☐AMEX

Card number _____Exp. Date_____

Card Holder Name_____Card Issue # _____

Signature _____Day Phone_____

☐ **BILL ME:** *(U.S. institutional orders only. Purchase order required.)*

Purchase order # _____
Federal Tax ID 13559302 • GST 89102-8052

Name_____

Address_____

Phone_____ E-mail_____

Copy or detach page and send to: **John Wiley & Sons, One Montgomery Street, Suite 1200,
San Francisco, CA 94104-4594**

Order Form can also be faxed to: **888-481-2665**

PROMO JBNND